AFRICAN AMERICAN

SEVENTH-DAY ADVENTIST HEALERS
IN A MULTICULTURAL SOCIETY

RAMONA L. HYMAN, PhD *and* ANDY LAMPKIN, PhD, EDITORS

Pacific Press®
Publishing Association
Nampa, Idaho | www.pacificpress.com

Cover design by Gerald Lee Monks
Cover design resources from gettyimages | Delmaine Donson
Inside design by Aaron Troia

The authors assume full responsibility for the accuracy of all facts and quotations as cited in this book.

You can obtain additional copies of this book by calling toll-free 1-800-765-6955 or by visiting AdventistBookCenter.com.

Scripture quotations marked AMP are from the Amplified® Bible, copyright © 2015 by The Lockman Foundation. Used by permission. (www.Lockman.org)

Scripture quotations marked ESV are from The Holy Bible, English Standard Version® (ESV®), copyright © 2001 by Crossway, a publishing ministry of Good News Publishers. Used by permission. All rights reserved.

Scripture marked GNV is from the 1599 Geneva Bible.

Scripture quotations marked KJV are from the King James Version.

Scripture quotations marked NASB are from the New American Standard Bible®, Copyright © 1960, 1971, 1977, 1995 by The Lockman Foundation. All rights reserved.

Scripture quotations marked NIV are from THE HOLY BIBLE, NEW INTERNATIONAL VERSION®. Copyright © 1973, 1978, 1984, 2011 by Biblica, Inc.® Used by permission. All rights reserved worldwide.

Scripture quotations marked NKJV are from the New King James Version®. Copyright © 1982 by Thomas Nelson. Used by permission. All rights reserved.

Scripture quotations marked NRSV are from the New Revised Standard Version of the Bible, copyright © 1989 by the Division of Christian Education of the National Council of the Churches of Christ in the USA. Used by permission. All rights reserved.

Library of Congress Cataloging-in-Publication Data

Names: Hyman, Ramona, editor. | Lampkin, Andy, 1967- editor.
Title: African American Seventh-Day Adventist healers / Ramona Hyman, PhD, editor, Andy Lampkin, editor.
Description: Nampa, Idaho : Pacific Press Publishing Association, 2021. | Includes bibliographical references. | Summary: "A history of African-American healers and the Seventh-day Adventist Church"— Provided by publisher.
Identifiers: LCCN 2021038303 | ISBN 9780816367849 | ISBN 9780816367856 (ebook)
Subjects: LCSH: General Conference of Seventh-Day Adventists--History. | African American Seventh-Day Adventists. | Race relations—Religious aspects—Seventh-Day Adventists.
Classification: LCC BX6153.2 .A39 2021 | DDC 286.7/32—dc23
LC record available at https://lccn.loc.gov/2021038303

September 2021

Dedication

This book is dedicated to our parents, Raymond R. Hyman, Annie D. Hyman, Olyen T. Lampkin, and Henrietta Lampkin, who labored beautifully bringing healing to many on earth's vineyard. Indeed, they are African American healers.

Contents

Our goal is to create a beloved community, and
this will require a qualitative change in our souls
as well as a quantitative change in our lives.
—Martin Luther King Jr.

Acknowledgment

African American Seventh-day Adventist Healers in a Multicultural Nation was conceived while we served in the School of Religion at Loma Linda University. A very special thank-you to Dr. Richard Hart, president of Loma Linda University; the School of Religion; and Loma Linda University Church for the foundational support provided to host the conference and the commemoration of Martin Luther King's idea of a "beloved community" where celebratory conversations can be held. You provided the soil out of which the idea could grow. Thanks to Dr. Edwin Hernandez, president of Advent-Health University for financially supporting the book project. A very heartfelt appreciation and thank you to Mrs. Isabel León for your unwavering wisdom and support of the project. And indeed, a very special thank-you to Drs. Willie and Eileen Davis, Dr. and Mrs. David Richardson, Mrs. Sharleen Lampkin, Madeia Jacobs, and Drs. David and Maxine Taylor for being the faith community that encouraged the dream.

Dr. Ramona L. Hyman and Dr. Andy Lampkin, editors

JON PAULIEN

Foreword

have been privileged to have engaged often with African American Seventh-day Adventists through the years—singing together in choirs, attending churches, sharing a common love for Scripture, working in ministry together. In all those encounters, I have been treated with amazing grace and hospitality despite the ways many of them had been treated by people who look like me. My life has been enriched by these many encounters, and I can truly testify that these relationships have had the kind of healing influence on me that this book is all about.

In the wake of the many protests that took place in the summer of 2020, I have had the opportunity to think more deeply about the black experience in America. Some of my white friends have wondered what it is about the black experience that is so uniquely troubling. After all, abuse, injustice, and attempts by one group to dominate others have been fairly universal in human experience. Even slavery of one kind or another has been the norm throughout most of human history. But what makes the legacy of slavery in America uniquely distasteful is that it was perpetrated in a country that claimed to be Jesus' shining city on a hill, a model and an example to other nations.

America was a child of the European colonial project, the first truly worldwide attempt to dominate others based on a sense of social and moral superiority. Europeans considered themselves superior because of their science; education; technology; and, yes, religion. The "white man's burden" was to lift up those who were inferior, those who had been left behind in all those Western advances in science and religion. But by feeling and acting superior, Europeans were unfaithful to the very gospel that had brought them so many blessings and so much prosperity. And like it or not, most of us born and raised in the European heritage were trained in a subtle sense of superiority. This training may not have been intentional; it was much more caught than taught. But nevertheless, it was very real. And my black brothers and sisters have felt the pain of that unstated judgment even when we did not. Unfortunately, Seventh-day Adventists have not been unaffected by this legacy.

America's Christian heritage makes the sins of slavery all the more reprehensible. Jesus said, "To whom much is given, from him much will be required" (Luke 12:48, NKJV). It is hard for me to grasp today that slavery and the lynching tree so often had the blessing of Protestant pulpits in the South. How could those who were taught to love even their enemies do such things to their neighbors? It goes to show how a sense of superiority can distort one's thinking. Whites are not inherently prone to sin's distortions, nor are blacks immune to them. The distortions of sin are common to us all. But in the aftermath of slavery and Jim Crow, some wrongs have not yet been righted. I have been less aware of that reality than I should have been.

In spite of marginalization, discrimination, and disrespect directed toward them largely based on the color of their skin, the black Seventh-day Adventists I have known have chosen not to return evil for evil but to respond to evil with good. They have chosen to heal rather than to hurt. They have chosen to live out the teachings and example of Jesus even when they received little or nothing in return. My church is so much the better for their gracious gift. To be a Seventh-day Adventist and not know the black Adventist story is to be incomplete. The book you are about to read is an important attempt to tell that story.

JOSEPH MCCOY

Foreword

A*frican American Seventh-day Adventist Healers* covers the water-front. It soars with the eagles and trots with the horsemen. It speaks the language of scholars and the lingo of the neighborhood. It underscores with legitimacy the DNA of the Seventh-day Adventist Church. It may not have been intentional, but the righteousness of Jesus boiling in their blood compelled the subjects of these essays to act without a thought of making headlines in newsprint or crawls at the bottom of a breaking-news television broadcast.

It makes us look at and evaluate with intensity the Black Lives Matter movement and compels us to act in either a protest march or with a mail-in ballot. It compels us to observe current social activity with renewed interest and determination to act with wisdom and make strides with precision.

From sermons to soliloquies, the essays in this book challenge us to go deeper into this important subject. As you read, you can almost see the healers become healed. The history that angers you as you read along will soften into a determination that does not fade into inaction.

James Kyle addresses the issues as a preacher physician who endured criticism for having the nerve to leave the clergy to become a doctor.

It sounded strangely like commentary heard when Barry Black dared to enter military chaplaincy. Andrea King speaks of stouthearted women who, with bravery unintended for headlines or highlight reels, lived the truth that makes us free. She shares the words of Isabella Baumfree, who, when recounting her flight to freedom with an infant child on her hip, said, "I did not *run* off, for I thought that wicked, but I *walked* off, believing that to be all right." Such words will propel you off your couch and not release you until you are walking with purpose with the people of the movement in the streets of this nation.

There is something about the action of early Adventist pioneers that makes you want to stand up and move to action. This book gives us seats in vehicles on the Underground Railway driven by Adventists. But most of all, it sounds an awakening trumpet for generations lulled to sleep by energy-robbing fantasy and mind-numbing illusions of expectancy from the "bubble of integration."

Maury Jackson opens the door for contextual healing. When understood, it should inspire the healing readers to look at the lives of healers who left the ranks because they were expected to minister in a multicultural nation without recognizing that there were social ills that needed to be addressed in the African American community—healers such as Sheaf; Humphrey; and the Mann brothers, who resisted until weary, worn, and tired, leaving a trail of souls ready for the kingdom. This is not to forget Irene Morgan Kirkaldy and Ruth Chambers, who were strong healers of the resistance.

Finally, there was Dr. Theodore Roosevelt Mason Howard, who attended Oakwood College, Union College, and the College of Medical Evangelists in Loma Linda, California. While working in Mississippi, he housed the mother of Emmitt Till, who had been brutally murdered, and the national black press that covered the trial of the murderers.

The parting and most relevant words in the book should ever ring in our ears: "Too often African American clergy (Adventist and non-Adventist) embrace the theological training handed down to them by white systematic theologians without questioning whether or not it rings true to their context; that is, does it 'apply' to their practices of healing the socio-spiritual ills?"

May Heaven's blessings accompany you as you journey through this inspiring work.

RAMONA L. HYMAN, PhD

Introduction

African Americans have played a critically indispensable role in shaping the American identity. As America's problematic immigrants (those whose American identity has been cast by slavery—what Peter Stamp calls the "peculiar institution"), African Americans have defined what it means to be a problematic immigrant whose citizenry and humanity have been interrogated and challenged because of the foundational emblem stamped on them through the institution of slavery. African Americans have lived, therefore, in the veiled consciousness of responding to a condition created by an economic and social institutional paradigm that has viewed them through a lens influenced by the horrid three-fifths compromise of 1787, a resolution that attempted to strip humanity from those Africans brought to America via the Atlantic slave trade. This attempted mutilation of the human spirit and black body has created human beings whose cognitive reality has called forth a group of people owning a racial sensitivity that has birthed generations of activists committed to creating an institutional paradigm in which equal and civil rights are collectively at its center. Moreover, the African American church has played a central role in creating an institutional civil rights platform. Examples abound of the civil rights stage from which the African American church has inspired a God-centered revolutionary practice. One such example is the Montgomery Bus Boycott of 1955. Rosa Parks's refusal to relinquish her seat to a white gentleman on Thursday, December 1, 1955, in Montgomery, Alabama, is legendary. The late Reverend Martin Luther King Jr.'s role as the leader of the boycott is also one of the famous stories associated with the boycott. However, the story must also include this: The Montgomery Bus Boycott was grounded in Christian ethos. On Monday, December 5, 1955, Christian preacher-servant Dr. King rose from the prophetic pulpit at the Holt Street Baptist Church to breathe into the imaginations of his church folk—people who would walk 382 days to end bus segregation in Montgomery, Alabama. He gave this inspiring message from the Christian point of view. King's *Stride Towards Freedom* affirms this. "In the first days of the protest . . . the phrase most often heard was 'Christian love.' "

Moreover, African American Seventh-day Adventists have also influenced America's religious, spiritual, and social discourse and, more specifically, the Seventh-day Adventist Church. The presence of the African people who suffered through what is historically known as the Middle Passage, chattel slavery, and Jim Crow segregation has encouraged the implicit formation of a people whose presence calls for the need of a holistically healed community to create what the late Dr. Martin Luther King Jr. deemed the "beloved society." The presence of enslaved Africans in America, who were deemed three-fifths of a human being, has also called forth the need for an institutional paradigm and conversation in which healing in relation to ethnicity and race must be the motif. One must affirm Delbert Baker's point when he says, "The SDA Church was to model Christ's gospel of love and inclusion—in practice. It was in this context that Ellen White repeatedly told church leaders that they were not fulfilling their mission if they neglected their disadvantaged Black brothers and sisters in their own country."[1]

Although psychologically, socially, and spiritually wounded because of being enslaved and dehumanized, the African American has successfully navigated these American shores and is the American institutional example of healing if one follows the definition of *health* as defined by the World Health Organization: A "state of complete physical, mental, and social well-being and not merely the absence of disease." Therefore disease can be, and often is, present in the psychological/social bloodline of an apparently healthy body, such as America and the church. The people who have encouraged the recognition of a discourse and conversation about race in America and, more directly, the Seventh-day Adventist Church are the African Americans. This complex conversation has influenced the church's multicultural paradigm. It has also established the need for an intellectual and communal conversation about the multifaceted contributions of African American Seventh-day Adventists.

The purpose of this collection of essays is to examine, highlight, and share the contributions and questions people of the African diaspora have gifted to the Seventh-day Adventist Church, America, and the world.

African American Seventh-day Adventist Healers in a Multicultural Nation is a collection of essays inspired by a celebratory conference sponsored by the School of Religion at Loma Linda University on February 16, 2013. The conference as well as the book project "fills a niche that is virtually untouched in the scholarly world," says Jon Paulien, former dean of the School of Religion at Loma Linda University. The purpose of this collection of essays is to examine, highlight, and share the contributions and questions people of the African diaspora have gifted to the Seventh-day Adventist Church, America, and the world. It also examines how they have, metaphorically speaking, been the agents of a poetic healing among those navigating the harsh reality of slavery and its aftermath.

The eight essays and sermons in this collection affirm the reality that African Americans have been healed by "something better." In addition to the traditional academic essay, the African American sermonic tradition is represented in the text. Moreover, what is clear about this collection of essays is a continuous need for an affirming dialogue about African Americans' contribution to America.

African American Seventh-day Adventist Healers in a Multicultural Nation includes the following essays:

1. "Faith Hall of Famers: Are We There Yet?" by Dr. Mervyn Warren. This sermon represents the testimonial sermonic tradition. Acknowledging Carter G. Woodson, the brain behind Black History Month, Warren asks a crucial question: "Are we there yet?" Offering the "main course" Hebrews 11:39, 40, Warren recognizes that "these were all commended for their faith, yet none of them received what had been promised, since God had planned something better for [the African Americans] so that only together with us would they be made perfect" (NIV).

2. "Repairers of the Breach: The Social Role of Black Religion," by Andy Lampkin. The black church emerged during the colonial period in the Southern United States at the intersection of spirituality and systemic oppression to serve the existential and spiritual needs of the black community. It began as clandestine gatherings away from the supervision of the ruling class. It emerged as a sanctuary for people without sanctuary, a place of caring and respite, an incubator for leadership development, and a location of social empowerment and spiritual renewal. Through its emancipatory practices, the church functions as a healing institution that has helped perfect the American republic. Considerable scholarly attention has been given to the significant role of the black church during the civil rights movement of the 1950s and 1960s. This

essay explores the emancipatory practices of the black church from antebellum times to our contemporary context. By exploring the unique contribution of black Seventh-day Adventists to the nation's healing, this essay fills a gap in the scholarly literature on the black church. Until recently, black Christians who were not a part of the nine traditional black denominations were neglected in the scholarly literature. This essay provides a foundation and context for understanding the unique contributions of black Seventh-day Adventists to healing the Seventh-day Adventist Church and the American republic as it explores how the black faithful live out their faith commitments amid oppression.

3. "We, Too, Sing America: African American Seventh-day Adventist Women Healers," by Andrea Trusty King. The Seventh-day Adventist Church is home to many exceptional African American women healers. This essay provides a survey of prominent African American women in Seventh-day Adventist history such as Sojourner Truth and Eva B. Dykes and others whose stories have gone untold, such as Jennie Allison and Lottie Blake. This essay describes their work and addresses the wounds these healers faced as African Americans and as Seventh-day Adventists. It discusses how race sometimes put these women in conflict with their denomination and how their gender put them in conflict with their race.

4. "Westward Leading: Healing Western Style; The African Diaspora Arrives in Compromised California Healing in a Free State," by Anthony Paschal. Initially, healing is rarely concerned with the morality of those needing healing. The healer is simply driven by a moral imperative to heal. Many a doctor has saved the life of a murderer, sewn him up, and released him to the proper process. Healing involves "having the goods, the evidence, and acting with mercy for the lifting up of the character of God." As the African diaspora spread from the west coast of Africa through an emotional, tumultuous, and successful journey to the West Coast of the United

States of America, this people demonstrated and continues to demonstrate resilience and resolve to "show the Lord's death [and Resurrection] till he come" (1 Corinthians 11:26, GNV). This essay explores what evangelizing and healing in a climate of hate and confusion means for Seventh-day Adventists, who see themselves as part of a "movement of destiny" preparing a people to meet God.

5. "To Dream, to Be, to Act: Healing a Sick Society," by James L. Kyle. As we witness the increasing physical and psychological sickness that has afflicted our society, how do African American Adventist physicians approach their calling in order to make a difference? This chapter focuses on the interplay of cherished dreams, self-realization, and spirit-driven action with the potential impact they can have on society. The dream, or calling, of the physician must first be realized in personal growth and character development. We cannot hope to change our society when we have not first experienced the change in our own being.

6. "Healing Shepherds and the Pastoral Care of African American Religioracial Ills," by Maury Jackson. Black theology is a practical theology. When African American clerics attempt to offer a healing word, that word should not begin in a context different from the context of those to whom they seek to minister. Nor should it be one that does not take seriously the lived experience of black people. Before taking up the task of being healers in a multicultural nation, pastors need to recognize that there are social ills in the African American community that must be addressed. The need for religioracial healing among African American people calls for the African American Adventist pastor-healer to (1) resource black theology as the conceptual framework for applying caring techniques, (2) replot the pan-African story to give voice to subversive memories of resistance, and (3) reimagine the Bible as a source for nurturing social solidarity.

7. "Healed by Something Better," by Calvin Rock. Rock's sermon

is testimonial and revelatory. The principle of "something better" is nestled in Hebrews 11:40 and is mentioned no less than eleven times in Hebrews's memorable portrayal of the means whereby Christ reconciles lost humanity. Likewise, history reveals that this principle, nestled in the human heart, is a true and traceable cause of humanity's most noble and productive energies.

8. "Conference Mission, Structure, and Function: An Analysis of Organizational Unity and Mission Particularity in the North American Division of the Seventh-day Adventist Church," by Leslie Pollard. This paper is an open invitation to conversation. Pollard illustrates both unity and autonomy within Seventh-day Advent-ist structure. The chapter demonstrates the way in which African American Seventh-day Adventists have woven culture and mission into an organizational arrangement that preserves connection to the worldwide Seventh-day Adventist church while translating the healing power of the SDA message into the cultural idiom of peoples of color. It is intended to provide a thoughtful examination of the organizational structures existing in the North American Division of Seventh-day Adventists (hereafter, NAD) that are offi-cially designated as "regional conferences." Recently, several writers and speakers have urged changes in the NAD that intend to dissolve the regional conference structure. These calls have been forwarded in the stated interest of "unifying" the Adventist Church in North America.

Given the amount of discussion generated in internet chat rooms, periodicals, websites, and in classrooms, it is helpful to initiate an open conversation that moves beyond the heat of assertions to the light of thoughtful consideration of biblical, theological, and missiological perspectives on some of the weightier questions raised by the continued presence of the regional conference structure in North America. Questions related to this discussion of mission and structure include, but are not limited to, the following: Does the New Testament require or mandate an ideal organizational structure? Do passages such as John 17:21; Ephesians 2:14–18; or Galatians 3:27, 28 demand identicality of structure? What role, if any, does or should gender, race, culture, ethnicity, and nationality play in Christian mission and community building? Are "ethnic" structures de facto violations of Christian unity? Should regional conferences be considered evidence of "race-based organizational segregation" in the Seventh-day Adventist Church? Should the creation of "ethnic" evangelism and congregations be discouraged or promoted? What is the biblical relationship between unity and diversity? And does the existence of state and regional conferences symbolize an ongoing divide between white and black Adventists in the United States?

Finally, if there are lessons to be garnered from this collection of essays, it is this: An authentic and celebratory dialogue about African Americans who have been systematically "othered" because of race needs to find its way onto the marquee of the Christian consciousness and into a systematic plan to implicitly improve race relations in the church and society.

Beautifully and intellectually, *African American Seventh-day Adventist Healers in a Multicultural Nation* is a call; it is a linguistic portrait of a people who James Cone says were put on "lynching trees" to die; however, they lived. If there are lessons to be garnered from this collection of brilliant essays, it is this: an authentic and celebratory dialogue about African Americans who have been systematically "othered" because of race needs to find their way onto the marquee of Christian consciousness and into a systematic plan to explicitly improve race relations in the church and society.

Ramona L. Hyman, PhD

Dr. Ramona L. Hyman is a writer, speaker, and professor "whose words are powerful memories for us to walk in the 21st century," says Sonia Sanchez. She is a graduate of Temple University (BA), Andrews University (MA), and earned her doctorate from the University of Alabama, Tuscaloosa. She is the author of *I Am Black America*. Of her literary work, African American critic, Dr. Joyce Joyce says, "Hyman challenges audiences to explore a poetic imagination grounded in a feel for the southern landscape, African-American literary and political history, Black spirituality, and a creative fusion of Black folk speech with a Euro-American poetic vernacular. Dr. Ramona L. Hyman emerges as a strong Black intellectual poetic voice." At present, Hyman is working on "Montgomery 55 on My Mind: Lessons From the Boycott," and "Jesus in Alabama," a collection of poetry.

---

1. Delbert W. Baker, "Black Seventh-day Adventists and the Influence of Ellen G. White," *Perspectives*, https://d34387f8-b80b-4319-a5ee-4b34617a2bab.filesusr.com/ugd/dc5cd6_2e21f03038694d25a9b90ca4c08d2326.pdf.

MERVYN A. WARREN, PhD, DMin

Faith Hall of Famers:
Are We There Yet?

Since 1976, February has been established as Black History Month, an outgrowth of the Black History Week begun by Carter G. Woodson back in 1926. Woodson, a professor at Howard University, was a black historian who had a PhD degree from Harvard University. He is generally credited with being the "father" of this type of observance that calls attention to bridges that heal.

In Hebrews 11:39, 40, we read: "These were all commended for their faith, yet none of them received what had been promised, since God had planned something better for us so that only together with us would they be made perfect" (NIV).

Who are the stalwarts here lifted to our view as prototypical patterns of faith and identified only as "these"? They are the three "waves of faith" champions mentioned earlier in Hebrews 11, beginning with the scratch name of Abel (verse 4, the first wave). Then comes the lead name of Gideon (verse 32, the second group). Wave 3 bears the nameless label of "others" (verse 35). Taking a holistic view of the entire chapter, we can imagine, if not visualize, all of the waves of faith running in a relay race, each sharing the baton within their group as well as passing it on to the next group. Finally, wave 3 delivers the baton to a fourth group bearing the nomenclature of "us" who, though not among the preceding "these" of verse 39, nevertheless are privileged with "something better," which comprehends running the anchor leg of the race and delivering the baton like champions across the victorious finish line of "perfection" described though not necessarily explained in verses 39 and 40.

If you read the entire chapter in one sitting, you will come away deeply blessed and impressed by a parade of compelling, robust personalities reminiscent, perhaps, of a post-Olympic procession. Reading this chapter, I get the thrill of strolling through an art gallery of exquisitely framed heroes and heroines of Scripture, some of whom I recall growing up with through childhood bedtime stories. On a more recent note, the gallery of Hebrews 11 takes me back to 2008 when I participated in the Martin Luther King Jr. Preachers' Hall of Fame induction ceremony at Morehouse College in Atlanta, Georgia. When inductees are led through the corridor where portraits of crown princes of gospel preachers (principally from the past) line the walls of that sacred space, one instantly senses their portraits mean something infinitely more than mere interior decoration or exterior publicity. Perhaps we can compare Hebrews 11 to something on the scale of a wax museum or the handsomely carved faces at Mount Rushmore, boldly modeling presidents Washington, Jefferson, Roosevelt, and Lincoln or the stunning memorial of Martin Luther King Jr. in the nation's capital.

One thing is for sure, whatever our image of the faith warriors from the pages of Hebrews, their exploits set the bar so high that they unwittingly come across as bigger than life. Intrepid Enoch! Majestic Moses! Gigantic Gideon! A daunting David! So superhuman, so "inhuman" in their humanness!

At any rate, have you ever wondered what it would take to get your name in the "Faith Hall of Fame"? Just thinking about it causes me to shrink back and whisper: "I'm not quite certain I am ready to face what these members of the biblical faith hall of fame went through.

Maybe I should settle for a discount, bargain-basement level of faith that doesn't cost so much. Would not a "cheap grace" brand be sufficient? I'm thinking about a caliber of faith that settles for "If I can just make it in, that's good enough for me."

> We must first become clear, unmistakably clear, that the playing field of Hebrews 11 has been leveled by nothing more, nothing less than the gift of faith.

Or is it? We must first become clear, unmistakably clear, that the playing field of Hebrews 11 has been leveled by nothing more, nothing less than the gift of faith—a faith that reaches beyond the veil (see Hebrews 6:19) and "takes hold of the arm of infinite power"[1] as Ellen White describes it. It is a faith that does not demand all the answers when faced with tough questions about justice and freedom and equality. The Southern preacher from Atlanta who became the conscience for our nation is credited with the statement, "Faith is the first step even when you don't see the staircase." Yet its mustard-seed size orders mountains to disappear and summons "justice" to "run down like water and righteousness like an ever-flowing stream" (Amos 5:24, AMP).

Faith in the flesh

"God had promised something better for us so that only together with us would they be made perfect" (Hebrews 11:40, NIV). Who are these special mortals identified as "us" and so favored with the promise of God? Where are they headed in the climactic stream of the members of the faith hall of fame? How does "something better" find a place in the picture?

I take my position with those interpreters who give this bold declarative an eschatological application, opening its arms wide and encircling post–New Testament Christians as well as those to whom the letter was first written. Our immediate perspective allows a representative roll call comprehending faith stalwarts all the way from the Waldenses to Martin Luther, from John Wesley and William Miller to J. N. Andrews, Joseph Bates, James and Ellen White, and others. Others, I submit, such as African American Seventh-day Adventists healers, sought and still seek a curative quality for our church. In Adventist theology, those making up the "us" faith company are accorded the sublime privilege of not merely joining the ranks of the faithful but also of being counted among the God-honored champions having the "faith of Jesus" inherent in the three angels' messages (Revelation 14:6–12).

The best of African American Adventist advocates past and present have refused to nitpick at our church but, rather, have exercised the option and obligation to address and redress areas of concern for the healing of the spiritual corporate body rather than to kill, steal, and destroy. It was Emil Brunner who said, "The chief sin of the church is that she frequently withholds the gospel from herself." The church is in the world, and thus, she does tend to reflect the society of which she is a part. While on the one hand, she congratulates herself for exalting the Ten Commandments, on the other hand, she has been found hiding conveniently behind civil law to excuse not practicing the spirit of the law of God—particularly in the realm of human relations on a real, personal level.

Ellen G. White and Martin Luther King Jr. may seem to have been collaborating when you consider that they spoke similar faith and strategy to men and women of flesh in the church and civil communities, although their ministries occurred in separate generations half a century apart. King demanded that "any law that demeans its citizens or violates the dignity of the human personality" must be challenged, albeit by peaceful means. His emphasis on the intrinsic worth of all human beings is a philosophical concept known as "personalism," which King studied under professors Edgar L. Brightman and

L. Harold DeWolf for his PhD program in systematic theology at Boston University. A surprising revelation for many of us resident in the Seventh-day Adventist Church is that Ellen White's ministry was a precursor to King's on this very matter of laws meting out injustice to fellow humans. Listen to her eloquent finality when she said: "When the laws of men conflict with the word and law of God, we are to obey the latter, whatever the consequences may be. The law of our land requiring us to deliver a slave to his master, we are not to obey; and we must abide the consequence of violating this law."[2]

That selfsame principle of human justice spoke out through the idea of the "two worlds" in which Langston Hughes of the Harlem Renaissance said African Americans live their day-to-day lives. African American Seventh-day Adventists find themselves obligated to try to bring healing to the church's systemic resistance against relating the Holy Place to the workplace, Christian justification to social justice, the truth that "all men are brothers" to the fear of becoming brothers-in-law, the biblical declaration that God made of one blood all nations (Acts 17:26) to the chicanery of the one-drop rule—that having just one drop of black blood in one's veins automatically negates the whole of the other drops.

Toward the finish line
Dr. Frank W. Hale Jr., president of Oakwood University from 1966 to 1971, served as vice provost of Ohio State University from the 1970s through the 1990s. During that tenure, he was instrumental in bringing acclaim to that university for awarding more PhDs among African Americans than any other university in the United States. If you ever visit the Ohio State University campus, you will see a handsome building named The Frank W. Hale Jr. Black Cultural Center. It is being enlarged to become the largest such center in the nation. Dr. Valerie Lee, the present vice provost of Ohio State University, is also a Seventh-day Adventist whose two sons and two

daughters were educated at Oakwood University in preparation for becoming healers rather than hinderers to their church and nation.

Back in 1961, Dr. Hale wrote a letter to a vice president of the General Conference of Seventh-day Adventists that summarizes the faith odyssey of African American healers in a brief paragraph:

> Elder _____,
>
> You are aware that I have been an Adventist since a child and plan to be, God helping me, until I die. I have accepted the doctrines and teachings of the Seventh-day Adventist Church much as I have accepted the Constitution of the United States. I do not debate either. . . . The laymen's movement is not an anti-church movement; it is anti-segregation and anti-discrimination.

The Hale statement to Seventh-day Church leadership might be interpreted but is probably not to be understood as a manifesto and certainly not as a threat. Hale intended to "heal," not hurt, encourage, not incite, because as a church, we all must contribute our faith part as members of a team charged with progressing the gospel of Jesus Christ toward ultimate victory.

Each team of the "Faith Hall of Fame" in Hebrews 11 has passed the baton of the gospel to the next group: Abel to Gideon (verses 4–32); Gideon to "others" (verses 32–35); "others" to "us"; and, finally, "us" to the finish line of God's purposes summarized by the victory wreath of "being made perfect"—perfect healing—individually and as the remnant church of God.

What shall we say more? In verses 1 and 2, I hear the team leader giving a pep talk to you and me as members of the eschatological last-day runners, "being made perfect" in the relay race of faith: "Therefore, since we are surrounded by such a great cloud of witnesses, let us throw off everything that hinders and the sin that so easily entangles. And let us run with perseverance the race marked out for us, fixing our eyes on Jesus, the pioneer and perfecter of our faith. For the joy set before him, he endured the cross, scorning its shame, and sat down at the right hand of the throne of God. Consider him who endured such opposition from sinners, so that you will not grow weary and lose heart" (Hebrews 12:1–3, NIV). Keeping the faith that works by love heals as nothing else can and gets us there.

Mervyn A. Warren, PhD, DMin

Mervyn A. Warren graduated from Dallas public schools; Oakwood University (BA); Andrews University, Seventh-day Adventist Theological Seminary (MA, MDiv); Michigan State University (PhD); and Vanderbilt Divinity School (DMin). He pastored and was ordained to the ministry in the Lake Region Conference. He retired from Oakwood University after serving as dean of Religion, vice president for Academic Affairs and Student Services, assistant to the president, provost and interim president. He is married to Barbara Moseley Warren and together they have two sons, two daughters, and eight grand-children.

---

1. Ellen G. White, Letter 12, 1901.
2. Ellen G. White, *Testimonies for the Church*, vol. 1 (Mountain View, CA: Pacific Press®, 1948) 201, 202.

ANDY LAMPKIN, PhD

Repairers of the Breach:
The Social Role of Black Religion

D uring Black History Month in 2013, a conference was convened
at Loma Linda University to explore the contributions of African
American Seventh-day Adventists (black SDAs) to the healing of
the church and the American republic. African Americans are the
oldest and only involuntary immigrant group in American society—
they were brought to this country as chattel. Since 1926, Americans
have annually recognized black history. Now, nearly a century since
the founding of black history celebrations, many have forgotten the
background of Black History Month. The ideal of black history began
in Chicago in the summer of 1915, when Carter G. Woodson traveled from Washington, DC, to Chicago to participate in a national
celebration of the fiftieth anniversary of the abolition of slavery.
Following his experience in Chicago, Woodson worked diligently
to get the experiences and accomplishments of African Americans
recorded in history.

To accomplish this task, he founded *The Journal of Negro History*
in 1916. A century later, this journal remains in circulation under
the title *Journal of African American History*. Woodson believed that
publishing the history and accomplishments of African Americans
would promote positive race relations in the United States and also

correct misconceptions and negative stereotypes about African Americans. Under the leadership of President Gerald Ford, as the nation celebrated its bicentennial in 1976, the national celebration of Black History Week was expanded to become Black History Month. President Ford encouraged all Americans to "seize the opportunity to honor the too-often neglected accomplishments of Black Americans in every area of endeavor throughout our history."[1] Since the mid-1970s, every American president has supported the annual theme of Black History Month.

The 2013 Loma Linda conference was held to complement the goals of Black History Month—highlighting the contributions of African Americans to society with a focus on black Seventh-day Adventists. This was no easy task. Never before had such an undertaking transpired. The approach was to situate black Seventh-day Adventists within the larger context of the Black Church tradition. Black Adventists are a part of the larger black community and, therefore, share the black religious traditions of American society. In this view, the historic Black Church is the context for understanding the contributions of African American Adventists to the church and American society.

In *Black Church Studies: An Introduction*, Stacey M. Floyd-Thomas et al. provide a good overview of the Black Church, its ontological status, epistemology, theological commitments, mission, and ministries. Black Church studies is a relatively new discipline in religious studies. It explores the history, development, and work of the Black Church. Black Church studies is proving to be an invaluable resource for understanding the social roles of black religion. Emerging at the intersection of spirituality and systemic oppression, the Black Church serves the spiritual and existential needs of black people. For African Americans, the Black Church became a vital place of worship, social empowerment, self-help, and racial uplift. For more than two centuries, the Black Church, both free and chattel, North and South, has been a resource for healing, care, respite, and spiritual renewal for the black faithful.

Prior to the legal recognition of the Black Church, it existed as a nascent institution in the shadows of slavery as an invisible entity. In bush arbors, hollows, and slave cabins, worshipers gathered, prayed, sang, testified, preached, and comforted each other. Beyond the supervision of the white ruling class, these clandestine meetings provided occasions for slaves to assemble and truly express themselves. These gatherings captured the essence of Jesus' words: "Come to me, all you who are weary and burdened, and I will give you rest" (Matthew 11:28, NIV). This nascent church emerged as a sanctuary for people without sanctuary, a place of care and respite, the location of social empowerment and spiritual renewal.

The civil rights movement of the 1950s and 1960s was a Black Church movement. Many of its leaders and financial supporters were members of the Black Church. Notable civil rights leaders such as Dr. King, Adam Clayton Powell, Ralph Abernathy, Barbara Jordan, Mahalia Jackson, Jesse Jackson, John Lewis, Andrew Young, Rosa Parks, and Joseph Lowery were all active members of the Black Church and were motivated by its values. The most noted civil rights leader, Dr. Martin Luther King Jr., provided eloquence and depth to the American civil rights movement, preaching powerfully moving sermons that called people to social activism. He dazzled America with his speech "I Have a Dream." Dr. King stands as a giant, a statesman, an engaging intellectual, and one of the best representatives of the Black Church tradition.

If Dr. King were alive today, I suspect that he would give glory to God for what he was able to accomplish during his lifetime and point to scores of unsung heroes on whose shoulders he stood. He would discuss the foundation of his resolve and the strength of his faith—the Black Church. Dr. King's gifts, talents, and preaching style all had their roots in the Black Church's traditions. The Black Church provided leadership training and deep spiritual values that influenced Dr. King to call the black community to social action during the

1960s. Social activism and social engagement are ongoing features of the Black Church tradition that date back to its early history. Blacks developed communal and kinship networks as a means to combat the deleterious forces of slavery and other forms of injustice.

Since the enslaved were barred from "institutional Christianity," they created their own religion—slave religion. This proto–Black Church was a mix, or syncretism, of traditional African religions and American Christianity. Slave religion emerged as a nonconfrontational protest and an act of resistance to the ruling class's racist ideology. White Christian ministers preached to the enslaved the virtues of meekness, docility, obeying one's master, and doing good work. Blacks resisted this doctrinal reinforcement of their oppression in meetings outside the control of whites. Floyd-Thomas asserts, "In such stolen moments, enslaved Black women, men, and children gradually wrested their humanity from the grip of inhumane bondage through their worship of the sacred."[2] The nascent Black Church emerged out of these secretive meetings as an institution born out of resistance to the evils and dehumanization of slavery to counter the assaults on black humanity. Members of Black Churches "consecrated themselves to the purpose of resisting, escaping when possible, and ultimately surviving enslavement on the plantation in the South."[3]

Beyond the plantation, African Americans also practiced Christianity in the antebellum north. Northern Black Churches were sincerely involved in the abolitionist movement. Black abolitionist preachers spoke out against the evils of slavery and racial discrimination. While the members of the invisible institution worshiped quietly and out of sight on southern plantations, in northern states, the visible church operated in plain sight. Both supported the enduring values of human dignity, freedom, justice, and equality and instilled racial pride among their members. During the late nineteenth and early twentieth centuries, the Black Church became an essential institution among African Americans, providing nurture, care, spiritual direction, moral guidance, culture, music, charity, aid, mutual support, and leadership development.

The Bible has been a vital aspect of African American thought and culture. The Bible serves a key social function and intersects with every aspect of African American culture. We hear the voice of the Bible in the preacher's lyrical sermons, in the songs of mass choirs, in the themes of black spirituals, and in upbeat gospel songs. In addition to these religious contexts, we can hear the voice of the Bible in rap lyrics, stories told in communal places, instructions given to youth, and in various protests, including the civil rights movement. For the Black Church, the Bible became an essential source of the community's understanding of God's act of liberation.

Vincent L. Wimbush, in *The Bible and African Americans: A Brief History*, provides clues to understand how black Americans came to appreciate and appropriate the Bible for their circumstances. In brief, the Bible functioned as a sort of a "language-world."[4] It provided rhetoric, images, and stories that helped to explain the black experience as well as provide moral guidance to respond to their oppression.

It's worth discussing early black contact with the Bible. Africans' encounters with the Bible date back to the fifteenth century. At that time, European missionaries traveled to Africa in an attempt to convert Africans to Christianity and "humanize" them. Europeans brought the Bible with them for their devotion and as a tool of socialization. For European missionaries, the Bible was an important part of their religious-cultural self-understanding and ideology offensives. The Bible, it was argued, was God's direct Word to, for,

34

and about them. It contained God's mandates regarding world order and conditioned their worldview. The Bible was their socializing agent, cultural road map, and ideological tool of oppression.

Africans thought European claims regarding the Bible were a bit excessive. For Africans, God pervaded everything, so they had little problem with the idea that God can be revealed in a book. However, the claim that the Bible was God's exclusive revelation and held universal authority troubled African sensibilities. The textualization of divine communication and limiting God's communication to a book were points of contention. Africans possessed their own ideas about God and brought their ideas to bear on the Bible. This should not be surprising, for when the Bible is introduced into a "new" culture, it is not always understood or embraced in the way those who introduce it plan. Even when the Bible is welcomed, claims about it are always filtered through an existing hermeneutical lens. This was indeed the case in early African encounters with the Bible.

During the eighteenth century, African Americans encountered the Bible on slave plantations in North America and at evangelical camp meetings. The emphasis on personal conversion and personal piety in evangelical preaching persuaded many. The evangelicals taught that faith was to be interpreted in light of reading the Bible and that each person had the freedom to interpret the Bible for himself or herself. This was liberating for blacks because it meant that they, too, could read the Bible freely and selectively—focusing on certain parts and ignoring others.

Blacks articulated their interpretations of the Bible in their own way—in songs, prayers, sermons, rituals, dance, testimonies, and speeches. The Bible came to represent a language-world that they could enter and manipulate in light of their oppression.[5] Blacks were attracted to the stories about the Hebrews "escaping from bondage, and those about the wondrous works, compassion, passion, and resurrection of Jesus."[6] They read and listened in excitement to the

35

oracles and "prophetic denunciations of social injustice and visions of social justice."[7]

The Bible became a medium of communication about life's challenges and enigmas. Speaking to their situation, the stories seized and freed their imagination. Bible interpretation was complex, dynamic, and fluid, not controlled by the literal words of the text. Their readings gave "voice to a people" and helped them "negotiate a hostile world."[8] Their encounter with the Bible on southern plantations provided an opportunity for them to interpret the text in light of their circumstances and make the Bible their own.

According to Wimbush, by the nineteenth century, African Americans began to read the Bible from a nationalist perspective. The language-world of the Bible helped them to cultivate arguments, ideas, and strategies for action to address their plight. Sermons, orations, exhortations, and addresses tended to reflect concerns about the evils of slavery and the plight of the people. Civil rights arguments were cast in biblical imagery and language. African Americans argued that their experience was an antitype of that of the ancient Hebrews. Blacks identified with the Hebrew people during their Egyptian bondage.

New Testament theology of the fatherhood of God and the brotherhood and sisterhood of humankind shaped their ethical vision. They often quoted Galatians 3:28, "There is neither Jew nor Greek, there is neither slave nor free, there is neither male nor female; for you are all one in Christ Jesus" (NKJV). The kinship and unity of all humanity affirmed their basic humanity—although the system of slavery through custom and law declared them less than human.

A couple of examples from the nineteenth and early twentieth centuries will prove helpful in understanding how the Bible was used and interpreted from a nationalistic perspective during this era. For instance, the official motto of the African Methodist Episcopal denomination was "God Our Father; Christ Our Redeemer; Man

Our Brother." This is reminiscent of Galatians 3:28. This may not seem like a big deal to a contemporary reader. But such a statement in the late nineteenth century was a radical affirmation of the brotherhood of all humankind. It functioned as a counterclaim to the view advanced by many that whites and blacks belonged to different races and that blacks were less than human. Early in the twentieth century, Dr. E. C. Morris stated at the National Baptist Convention: "We early imbibed the religion of the white man; we believed in it; we believe in it now. . . . But if that religion does not mean what it says, if God did not make of one blood all nations of men to dwell on the face of the earth, and if we are not to be counted as part of that generation, by those who handed the oracle down to us, the sooner we abandon them or it, the sooner we will find our place in a religious sect in the world."[9] David Walker exclaimed: "All persons who are acquainted with history, and particularly the Bible . . . are willing to admit that God made man to serve Him alone . . . that God Almighty is the sole proprietor or master of the whole human family. . . . God will not suffer us, always to be oppressed. Our suffering will come to an end, in spite of all the Americans this side of eternity. Then we will want all the learning and talents among ourselves, and perhaps more, to govern ourselves.—'Every dog must have its day,' the American's is coming to an end."[10]

What is interesting about these readings is how the Bible is referenced as the foundation for their position regarding equality. In their interpretive schema, the Bible provides an interpretative framework for thinking about their experience as oppressed people in America. Embedded in their framework are the grounds for critiquing the system of American slavery and oppression. Their reading of the Bible and the liberation that they found in it provided a vision of a better set of circumstances. Again, these statements affirm African American humanity.

Allen Dwight Callahan, in his book *The Talking Book: African*

Americans and the Bible, also explores black American readings and appropriations of the Bible. He agrees with Wimbush that the Bible is an important resource in African American life and culture. In his work, he offers four biblical motifs that emerged and remain essential features of African American Christian faith and practice: exile, exodus, Ethiopia, and Emmanuel.[11] We will briefly explore the biblical motifs of exile and exodus.

African Americans, borrowing from the Bible, understood themselves to be a people in exile—reminiscent of the children of Israel during their Babylonian captivity. At times, black Americans reflected on their experiences and would reference Psalm 137:1–4,

By the rivers of Babylon—
  there we sat down and there we wept
  when we remembered Zion.
On the willows there
  we hung up our harps.
For there our captors
  asked us for songs,
and our tormentors asked for mirth, saying,
  "Sing us one of the songs of Zion!"

How could we sing the LORD's song
  in a foreign land? (NRSV).

This communal lament captures the hopelessness that is often felt by exiles, captive and estranged from the familiarity of their homeland. The pain of being taunted is expressed, as is the utter insult of the situation. This is how many African Americans must have felt, being powerless and considered chattel in a land of freedom. Frederick Douglass, perhaps one of the most well-known spokesmen for the black community during the era, evoked the lament of Psalm

137 in his denunciations of slavery in 1852. During a Fourth of July address titled "The Meaning of July Fourth," he denounced the hypocrisy of a national celebration of freedom in a land of slavery. He exclaimed, "This Fourth of July is yours, not mine. . . . You may rejoice; I must mourn." Douglass references parts of Psalm 137 but expresses it in his own voice:

> "By the rivers of Babylon, there we sat down. Yea! We wept when we remembered Zion. . . . O Jerusalem let my right hand forget her cunning. If I do not remember thee, let my tongue cleave to the roof of my mouth."
>
> Fellow-citizens, above your national, tumultuous joy, I hear the mournful wail of millions! whose chains, heavy and grievous yesterday, are, to-day, rendered more intolerable by the jubilee shouts that reach them. If I do forget, if I do not faithfully remember those bleeding children of sorrow this day, "may my right hand forget her cunning, and may my tongue cleave to the roof of my mouth!" To forget them, to pass lightly over their wrongs, and to chime in with the popular theme, would be treason most scandalous and shocking, and would make me a reproach before God and the world.[12]

Douglass identified the cries of black people with the ancient blues of lament of the Hebrew people. A critique of the oppressors who perpetrate harm against fellow human beings is embedded in Douglass's lament. He also charges the oppressed to never forget their experience of oppression. If they do forget the suffering of those who have experienced oppression, let pain and suffering follow such forgetfulness. Forgetfulness is an offense to God and devalues the experience of the sufferers. God is the Liberator of black slaves just as He was the Deliverer of the Israelites from Egyptian bondage. The historical plight of African Americans has been the plight of all exiles; that is, of being a people without a place or respite.

The biblical metaphor of exile would eventually break down, as it describes the African American experience only to a degree. Their exile was completely different from that of the Israelites; it was permanent. Egypt was on both sides of the Red Sea. That is to say that oppression was on both sides of the Emancipation Proclamation. Oppression morphed from chattel to Jim Crow segregation with repressive black codes whose main goal was to limit African American flourishing.

African Americans were selective in the biblical texts they used to reflect on their exile. There was a preference for Ezekiel 37, the prophet Ezekiel's discussion of exile in his vision of dry bones. For the ancient Hebrew people, this vision represented life after death and a collective resurrection. For African Americans, Ezekiel's vision was emblematic of African American hopes. Sermons of this era use the imagery of Ezekiel 37 to stress the brokenness of a life of slavery. Evoking Ezekiel's vision of dry bones has an additional benefit in that it avoids providing explanations or reasons for the exile. Other biblical texts, such as Jeremiah 32:40, offer that the exile is punishment for Israel's sin and a lack of piety. However, in Ezekiel, there is a collective resurrection, and the issue of sin is not addressed. The resurrection of the dead is an exercise of divine favor for an oppressed people. God simply acts to right a wrong. Ezekiel's vision was attractive because it avoided victim blaming—blaming the oppressed for their oppression. This was an important feature as African Americans were combating the racist ideology that their enslavement was the will of God as divine punishment for sin—the curse of Ham, practicing African traditional religions, or a myriad of other unsubstantiated reasons.

If Callahan and others are correct, African Americans read the story of the Exodus more than any other biblical story. In this story, African Americans saw their own aspirations for freedom from bondage. The Exodus narrative was used as a biblical indictment against slavery.

Exodus provided an argument that God was opposed to slavery and that He would eventually judge America for its crimes against humanity.

David Walker, an African American abolitionist and writer, evoked the Exodus narrative to express the excessive brutality of the American slave regime. He is worth quoting at length: "We . . . are the most wretched, degraded, and abject set of beings that ever lived since the world began and [. . .] the white Americans having reduced us to the wretched state of slavery, treat us in that condition more cruel (they being an enlightened and Christian people) than any heathen nation did any whom it had reduced to our condition."[13] Worse than the injury of servitude was the added insult of the refusal of whites to recognize the slaves as human beings. Walker adds, "Show me a page of history, either sacred or profane, in which a verse can be found, which maintains, that the Egyptians heaped the insupportable insult upon the children of Israel, by telling them they were not of the human family. Can whites deny this charge? Have they not, after having reduced us to the deplorable condition of slaves under their feet, held us up as descending originally from the tribes of Monkeys or Orang-Outangs? O! My God! I appeal to every man of feeling—is not this insupportable?"[14]

The ancient Hebrews in Egyptian bondage paralleled their experience as captives with desperate hopes of emancipation.

African American thinkers often evoked the biblical motif and narrative of Exodus. The ancient Hebrews in Egyptian bondage paralleled their experience as captives with desperate hopes of emancipation. Walker suggests that the American system of slavery was the worst in human history, much more brutal and vicious than that of Egyptian slavery or any other slave regime that has existed. In his view, the system was so brutal and oppressive that not even God has witnessed such brutality and oppression. This is a powerful rhetorical claim.

As the system of slavery was collapsing, "racialized" science became more prominent. Science was put into the service of racism and racial bigotry, and claims were made that blacks were not a part of the human family. American scientists sought to provide a justification for slavery by reducing black Americans to nonhuman descendants of the great apes. A unique and enduring feature of the American slave system was its viciousness and dehumanizing elements. Walker addresses the dehumanization and claims against black humanity. Many attempts were made to defend such a specious claim.

The Exodus narrative was a significant resource for African Americans' reflection on their circumstances. However, the corresponding biblical language of "the Promised Land" was not so prominent. Blacks did not see America as a "Promised Land." They were captives and exiles in a strange land. For them, America was Egypt and/or Babylon—not the Promised Land. Moreover, the European settlers of America had already evoked the Promised Land motif to carry out their agenda of manifest destiny, which justified the perpetual subjection of blacks and, in addition, led to the extermination of the Amerindians.

The nascent Black Church emerged at the intersection of spirituality and systemic oppression to attend to the spiritual and existential needs of black people. The Black Church became an important place of worship, social empowerment, self-help, and racial uplift. The Bible emerged as its essential resource, a "talking book"; exploration into its language-world helped to explain the African American experience. In the Bible, they found stories and language that paralleled and spoke to their experience as an oppressed people in America. In addition, they found reasons to hope as God worked on behalf of the oppressed and captive. Biblical themes prompted a self-understanding of who they were as a people of God. The liberating motifs they found in the Bible bolstered their claims to be God's people and informed their view that God was with them. As they heard stories of how God delivered people from captivity, they found a liberator God who was neither complacent nor complicit in their oppression.

Black Americans appropriated the biblical text in very sophisticated ways that affirmed their humanity. They gleaned from the Bible the inherent worth and dignity of all persons and the brotherhood and sisterhood of all humanity. Through the language-world of the Bible, they affirmed important aspects of their humanity and understood themselves as equal in dignity and worth to all other human beings. Affirming their humanity, they launched the fight for their human rights and, later, their civil rights. Their self-identification as God's people provided them courage and the arguments to sustain the movement to be free from chains and other forms of oppression.

This emancipatory hermeneutical schema remains at work in the Black Church and community today. For the past few decades, black Americans have been earning PhDs in religion from the nation's most prestigious institutions of higher education. This emerging community of black scholars of religion has offered us an even more enriched understanding of African American biblical, theological, and ethical analysis through the lens of scholarship.

Among the latest trends in modern biblical and theological studies are black theology and womanist theology. These two hermeneutical frameworks further capture and expand on the essence of African American clergy and laypersons' hermeneutics. These scholars explore in very careful, systematic, and nuanced ways African American approaches to the biblical text.

Black theology saw liberation as the primary focus of the Christian faith, expressed in its original formulation in four main features: (1) Jesus was identified as the "oppressed One" whose ministry on earth was primarily liberation of oppressed people; (2) God takes on the identity of the oppressed; (3) God is presented as black since it was black Americans who experienced oppression; and (4) authentic Christian faith works on behalf of the oppressed; anything less is an affront to God. Black theology thrives in theological circles. Most theological seminaries and schools of religion teach the ideas of the seminal figures in black theology. Many Black Churches embrace the emancipatory hermeneutic of black theology and its call for social ministries.

Womanist theology is another movement in theological circles that has caught its stride. Womanist theology is a critique of traditional theology, black theology, and feminist theology. The womanist lens is focused on the intersection of race, gender, and class. Patriarchy is the focus of much of its critique. It also critiques the theological discourse of white women. Although white women theologians and biblical scholars have critiqued patriarchy, they tend to ignore and neglect the experience and the plight of black women. Black women confront the triple threat of sexism, racism, and classism. As a constructive proposal, womanist theological discourse seeks to advance the welfare and wholeness of the entire black community. Its typical theological themes include human dignity and the fullness of life.

In a general sense, black theology and womanist theology are both forms of liberation theology. Black theology seeks the complete and absolute liberation of black people in America. Womanist goals are, perhaps, more modest: seeking the "survival and quality of life" of black Americans. One should not make too much of the distinction between the two discourses; they are not antithetical to each other. Womanist thought, to be sure, is a corrective of the limitation of black male theological thinking, yet when operationalized among the black faithful, both seek the flourishing of African American people. It is difficult to determine the extent to which these two approaches have influenced the Black

Church. These are academic discourses that are debated among educated elites. Suffice it to say, however, these ideas have affected a generation of educated men and women in biblical and theological studies. As such, this theological discourse is finding its way to the Black Church and will influence generations of Black Faithful.

The preceding discussion demonstrates that since its inception on southern plantations, the Black Church has taken on social roles. Black religion has not, and cannot be, focused solely on issues of transcendence and otherworldliness to the neglect of the real-life experience of black people or of what is actually happening in black communities. Black Churches have acted, and must act, to ameliorate the harm of racist oppression and remain committed to the flourishing of blacks in American society.

Black Seventh-day Adventists cannot avoid their fate of being black and Christian in America, which requires, indeed demands, that they reflect theologically from the existential position of being a black in America. Black religion, even among Seventh-day Adventists, must take on a social role if it is to be faithful to its own traditions and if it is to practice faith on this earth. To be sure, some black Adventists have worked much more than others to improve the plight of blacks and to "perfect" the American republic. Those who have sought to "perfect" America have done so from a black perspective. Although black Seventh-day Adventists have not always embraced the historic Black Church and the historic Black Church has not always embraced black Seventh-day Adventists, the social ministries of both have been motived by deep theological commitments to liberate and work on behalf of the survival quality of God's people.

C. Eric Lincoln and Lawrence Mamiya are correct in suggesting that "as the only stable and coherent institutional area to emerge from slavery, Black Churches were not only dominant in their communities but they also became the womb of black culture and a number of major social institutions."[15] The Black Church emerged as a life-giving institution that stood as a foil to resist the evils of slavery and the dehumanization of black people. The historical and contemporary work of the Black Church, with its mission of social activism, seek the flourishing of black people.

All too often, the demands of modern life encourage us to look forward and not to reflect back on the journey. However, the Black Church has taught us to reflect on these words: "If it had not been for the Lord, where would I be?" The Black Church has left us a tremendous inheritance. Despite the circumstances of oppression, whether it was slavery, reconstruction, or Jim Crow segregation, the Black Church acting out of deep moral convictions responds to the needs of hurting people. It has bequeathed a tradition of spirituality, care of the soul, practices of healing, and social advocacy. This must be a part of the inheritance we pass on to future generations.

Andy Lampkin, PhD

Dr. Andy Lampkin is a Seventh-day Adventist minister and educator. He is currently Professor of Religion and Bioethics at AdventHealth University. He has also served as professor of religion at Oakwood and Loma Linda universities. He lectures and presents on various topics in religion and biomedical ethics. He earned an undergraduate degree at Oakwood University, and Masters and Doctor of Philosophy Degrees at Vanderbilt University in Ethics and Society.

---

1. History.com editors, "Black History Month," History.com, updated January 28, 2021, https://www.history.com/topics/black-history/black-history-month.

2. Stacey Floyd-Thomas, Juan Floyd-Thomas, Carol B. Duncan, Stephen G. Ray Jr., Nancy Lynne Westfield, *Black Church Studies: An Introduction* (Nashville: Abingdon Press, 2007), 13.

3. Floyd-Thomas et al., 12.

4. Vincent L. Wimbush, *The Bible and African Americans: A Brief History* (Minneapolis: Fortress, 2003), 4.

5. Wimbush, 7.
6. Wimbush, 24.
7. Wimbush, 24.
8. Wimbush, 30.
9. Wimbush, 40.
10. Wimbush, 44.
11. See Allen Dwight Callahan, *The Talking Book: African Americans and the Bible* (New Haven: Yale University Press, 2006), ix–xiv.
12. Callahan, 50, 51.
13. Callahan, 130.
14. Callahan, 130, 131.
15. C. Eric Lincoln and Lawrence H. Mamiya, *The Black Church in the African American Experience* (Durham: Duke University Press, 1990), 17.

ANDREA TRUSTY KING, DMin

We, Too, Sing America

African American Seventh-day Adventist Women Healers

There are things that make me proud to be an African American Seventh-day Adventist Christian. I am proud to say that the first president of the General Conference, John Byington, was a staunch abolitionist. He used his Bucks Bridge home as a stop for the Underground Railroad, and he often hosted fugitive slaves and Native Americans at his own table.[1] John P. Kellogg, another Adventist pioneer and father of Dr. John Harvey Kellogg, also ran an Underground Railroad station on his farm in Michigan.[2] Perhaps it was such forward-thinking people, in addition to their rightly dividing the Word of God, that attracted women like Sojourner Truth, an itinerant preacher, abolitionist, activist, and healer to the Advent movement. She was baptized into the Seventh-day Adventist Church by Uriah Smith.[3]

Originally named Isabella Baumfree, Sojourner Truth was bounced from plantation to plantation until she decided to escape with her infant child one year before slavery was abolished in New York. Of her escape she recalled, "I did not run off, for I thought that wicked, but I walked off, believing that to be all right."[4] After slavery had been abolished in New York, her son was sold to a slave owner in Alabama. She fought to get him freed by suing the owner. She won the case, becoming the first black woman to win a court case against a white man.[5]

She refused to settle merely for her own freedom or the freedom of her children. She went on to fight for the freedom of both women and blacks. She gave herself the name Sojourner Truth, for she believed that this name encapsulated the calling God had placed on her life to preach against slavery. Like Harriet Tubman, Sojourner Truth made several trips to the South to free slaves through the Underground Railroad.[6]

Sojourner Truth was an encourager and liberator of both great and small. When Frederick Douglass was speaking of the horrors of slavery in Boston, it appeared that he was quite discouraged. Hopelessness was beginning to creep into his speech and his heart. Sojourner Truth yelled from the front row, "Frederick, is God dead?"[7] This inspired and invigorated the whole audience. Her influence also earned her an invitation to the White House, where she met President Abraham Lincoln.[8]

She spoke at least twice at Millerite camp meetings in 1843.[9] She chronicles in her narrative how upon her arrival, everyone seemed to be so agitated and excitable—stricken with fear. This was understandable because, according to their calculations, the world was very soon to end. She'd speak to them to calm their minds, sing to them to give peace. When she moved to Battle Creek, she became friends with Ellen White.[10] She was a healer. This African American healer was able to operate with ease in various circles—from the Battle Creek Sanitarium to the White House; from the circles of black Frederick Douglass to Ellen Gould White. She was a healer.

In 1851, Sojourner Truth attended the Women's Rights Convention in Akron, Ohio. Watching this "tall, gaunt black woman in a gray dress and white turban, surmounted with an uncouth sunbonnet, march deliberately into the church, walk with the air of a queen up the aisle, and take her seat upon the pulpit steps"[11] caused quite a stir in the convention. Throughout the sessions, she perched herself like a statue, leaning against the wall while sitting on the steps.[12] As an entrepreneur, Sojourner Truth would sell her book, *Life of Sojourner Truth*, during intermission—an awesome feat because she could neither read nor write. When she wasn't selling, she was back on her step.[13]

While listening to the presentations, she heard how women were dainty and should be helped into carriages and lifted over ditches. A man announced at the convention that women should have the best place. Other speakers and women had choice seats, yet she was seated on the steps. The irony and hypocrisy of this moment were not lost on her. Her life as a woman included none of the womanly amenities.

Francis Gage, the president in charge of the convention, was warned not to let Truth speak. The organizers for women's rights did not want their cause muddied with abolition. Gage recalls, "Again and again, timorous and trembling ones came to me and said, with earnestness, 'Don't let her speak, Mrs. Gage, it will ruin us. Every newspaper in the land will have our cause mixed up with abolition and niggers, and we shall be utterly denounced.' "[14]

Gage was still undecided on whether she would allow Truth to speak. But after some male preachers from several denominations came and made light of the women's cause, Sojourner Truth could scarcely hold her seat. The men asserted that women were weak and that men had superior intellect. Furthermore, Jesus Christ, the Savior, was a man, and Eve, the first sinner, was a woman. No one wanted to rebut what was being said. Most women were too timid to speak out in the meetings. Sojourner Truth, however, was not afraid.

She rose and made her way to the front, exciting quite a commotion. People continued to beg Gage to not allow her to speak. Gage, too, arose and quieted the audience. She then announced Sojourner Truth. Truth's speech was masterful and memorable and arguably the only reason we remember the Akron, Ohio, Women's Rights Convention of 1851.

Truth would address women's rights, but her immediate priority was to let her hearers know that she was included in this category. It became clear to Sojourner Truth that they had no intention of offering her, a black woman, the rights they were fighting to gain for themselves. Thus, her first order of business was to remind them that she was a woman too:

> "That man over there says that women need to be helped into carriages, and lifted over ditches, and to have the best place everywhere. Nobody ever helps me into carriages, or over mud-puddles, or gives me any best place! And ain't I a woman? Look at me! Look at my arm! I have ploughed and planted and gathered into barns, and no man could head me! And ain't I a woman? I could work as much and eat as much as a man—when I could get it—and bear the lash as well! And ain't I a woman? I have borne thirteen children and seen most all sold off to slavery, and when I cried out with my mother's grief, none but Jesus heard me! And ain't I a woman?"[15]

After first establishing her right to be there as a woman, she then tackled the task at hand and provided an adept rebuttal for women's rights. Equipped with a brilliant mind, she turned every point used against women's rights on its head and used it in their favor. "If the first woman God ever made was strong enough to turn the world upside down all alone," she proclaimed, "these women together ought to be able to turn it back, and get it right side up again! And now they is asking to do it, the men better let them."[16]

Sojourner Truth was just one of many exceptional African American women healers. Women like Anna Knight, the first female missionary to India and also the first black female employee of the Seventh-day

Adventist Church, were also healers.[17] Anna Knight learned about Seventh-day Adventists through mail correspondence as a young teenager. Because there were no schools in Mississippi for blacks, she devoured any reading material she could get her hands on. As Knight learned more about the Bible, she found that local pastors and the itinerant preachers who would come through her town knew so little of the Bible that she made a commitment to herself to get a formal education.[18] Knight eventually ended up at Battle Creek College, where she studied to be a nurse. There Knight took an oath before John Harvey Kellogg, the director of the Battle Creek Sanitarium, that she would use her training to serve others and not to make money. Upon completion of her nursing degree, Knight went back to Mississippi to start a school for African American children. There were many who were less than excited about her teaching blacks, and she often had to go to and from the school with a pistol for her safety.[19]

Kellogg had invited Knight to be a delegate for the General Conference session in Battle Creek. There she heard of the need for nurses to go to India as missionaries. Knight decided to go if the denomination would send two people to continue the work at her school in Gitano, Mississippi. She made the thirty-day journey to India and worked tirelessly teaching, selling books, and working in the fields to raise money for the school. Knight worked so hard in the field one day that she fainted and did not wake up for three days.[20]

While in India, Knight got word that the work in Mississippi had been abandoned. The school had been burned down, and everyone who tried to continue the work in the black school was threatened. When Knight received a letter from one of her former students asking why she was in India trying to convert the heathen when her own people were growing up in Mississippi as heathens, her heart was broken. Knight wrote to the General Conference pleading for them to send someone to Mississippi to work with the students there. If they would not, she requested a furlough so that she could do it herself. They decided to grant her a furlough.[21]

When her furlough came, Knight made her way back to Mississippi. Almost immediately, she started a school with twenty-two students. Knight organized the first Seventh-day Adventist group in south-central Mississippi. After holding services on Saturday in her home, she would walk six miles to Soso, Mississippi, and teach a Sabbath School class of fifty to eighty adults. Knight would teach them the Sabbath School lesson from *Our Little Friend*, and they loved it.[22]

Some in the town thought a woman shouldn't preach. Knight recalls their threats: "This here woman has gone up North and got all these Northern ideas, and is bringing all this in here and getting these people stuck up, and trying to preach, going from one place to another holding meetings there and here. We will fix her."[23] They threatened to catch her on the road and kill her. This was not the first time Knight was threatened, nor was it the first time she refused to back down. Knight (with her pistol) had an undying commitment to God and healing, whether in the fields of India, the schools of Mississippi, or the sanitariums of the South.

Anna Knight is an inspiration to women in ministry. Although she is hailed as an educator, she was a minister and a preacher. Knight pastored and organized churches even though she was not recognized formally by the denomination for doing so. Anna Knight is a predecessor for women in ministry who now release healing to this new generation. She was the first African American woman to be hired by the Seventh-day Adventist Church. Knight was a sought-after speaker in churches and universities across denominational lines and trained pastors at union workers' meetings.[24]

> Knight (and her pistol) had an undying commitment to God and healing, whether in the fields of India, the schools of Mississippi, or the sanitariums of the South.

Anna Knight served in the Southeastern Union, which covered Florida, Georgia, North and South Carolina, and eastern Tennessee, as the associate Home Missionary secretary, Missionary Volunteer secretary, and educational secretary for the union. She was charged with "looking after the work in the colored churches and schools." Knight later served in the Southern Union, which covered Kentucky, western Tennessee, Mississippi, Alabama, Louisiana, and western Florida. When the two unions combined, she was called to the same positions over the entire territory and was again tasked with looking after the work of the colored people.[25]

What Anna Knight did for the colored work, a corresponding male was doing for the white work. She had a clergy pass for her travel, by which some could conclude that the transportation industry recognized her as clergy—although her own denomination did not. Knight was not ordained but carried a missionary's license.[26] This was because she was a woman. As Josephine Benton points out, "Any man carrying her responsibilities year after year would surely have been designated a minister and would have been ordained."[27]

Knight was no stranger to sexism and racism in the church. Though she did not often talk about it publicly, Knight lived with this bitter reality from childhood. She recalls, "I had thought Adventists were saints. When I found they were real human beings, it was an awful disappointment. But I believed the truth nevertheless."[28]

Anna Knight worked in the Southern Union with black churches and schools. When regional conferences (black conferences organized by regions) were instituted in 1945, her office was eliminated. Knight was offered a job in both the South Atlantic and the South Central Conferences. Although she did serve in interim positions in both conferences as they were getting started, Knight decided that it was a good time to retire. She had worked tirelessly for the Lord and for the church for decades and was already in her seventies.

Anna Knight placed her commitment to God first and foremost in her life. She also honored the commitment she made before Kellogg to help people instead of making money. While doing union work, Knight would make sure that she personally gave an annual physical exam to each black student attending Adventist schools in the Southern Union—an admirable feat and a much-needed one because many African Americans had no other health care. When Knight retired in 1946, she reported that she had attended 9,388 meetings, made 11,344 missionary visits, written 48,918 letters, and traveled 554,439 miles.[29] A building named after Knight stands on the Oakwood University campus in her honor—as a monument to her work as a missionary, an educator, and a nurse. Anna Knight was a healer.

Others, such as a young, black Seventh-day Adventist woman named Irene Morgan, were looking for healing. She had recently suffered a miscarriage and had been visiting with her mother. Morgan was returning home on the Greyhound bus to Baltimore to see her doctor. She was seated in the last four rows of the bus, which were designated for blacks. The bus was filling up, and the driver told the blacks to go to the back. Thirty minutes into the ride, a white couple boarded, and the driver told Morgan and her seatmate to go to the back of the bus. She refused. A mother with an infant in her arms, seated next to Morgan, stood to go to the back. Morgan snatched her back to her seat. Infuriated, the bus driver drove straight to the jail in Saluda, Virginia. The driver got the sheriff, who threatened to arrest Morgan—to which she replied, "That's perfectly all right."[30] The sheriff produced a warrant for her arrest. Morgan took the "warrant," tore it up, and threw it out the window. She knew it was fraudulent because they didn't even know her name.

At this blatant disregard for his authority, the sheriff tried to physically remove Morgan from the bus. She kicked him in the genitals. In a *Washington Post* interview, she recalls: "He touched me. . . . That's when I kicked him in a very bad place. He hobbled off, and another one came on. He was trying to put his hands on me to get me off.

I was going to bite him, but he was dirty, so I clawed him instead. I ripped his shirt. We were both pulling at each other. He said he'd use his nightstick. I said, 'We'll whip each other.' "[31]

Eventually, the two men were able to get Morgan off the bus and into the jail. She pled guilty to resisting arrest and paid the one-hundred-dollar fine but refused to plead guilty for violating the segregation law or pay the ten-dollar fine. The Constitution forbade segregation in interstate commerce. Virginia and other southern states had long ignored the "commerce clause" and enforced racial segregation. Morgan's case went all the way to the United States Supreme Court and was argued by NAACP lawyers Thurgood Marshall and William Hastie. She won the case, and her victory became the catalyst for the freedom rides of 1947. The freedom riders would be heard shouting, "Get on the bus, sit any place / 'Cause Irene Morgan won her case!"[32]

Over a decade before Rosa Parks was thrown off the bus in 1955, Irene Morgan fought and won against segregation in interstate travel. In 2001, Morgan was awarded the Presidential Citizen's Medal by Bill Clinton. In the president's speech, he recognized her for her "quiet and brave fight for freedom." She fought "with dignity and determination."[33] The citation for her medal read, "When Irene Morgan boarded a bus for Baltimore in the summer of 1944, she took the first step on a journey that would change America forever."[34] She was on her way to a doctor's appointment, seeking healing. Little did she know, that day, she would be transformed into a healer.

When Lucille Byard, another black Adventist woman from New York, needed healing, her story did not have such a happy ending. She had been ill, but as a loyal Seventh-day Adventist, she wanted to be treated in an Adventist facility, for she believed its care would be superior to the New York hospitals. She made prior arrangements and took a train from New York to Maryland and then a taxi to the Washington Sanitarium. Upon arrival, Mrs. Byard filled out her paperwork and was admitted. She and her husband were both mixed with black and white parentage and were often mistaken for white.[35]

When the hospital workers saw that her paperwork said she was black, she was refused treatment. She was rolled out into a drafty corridor in the dead of winter. Her husband was told she needed to go across state lines to the Freedman's Hospital at Howard University, where blacks were treated. He begged for his wife to be treated at Washington Sanitarium because she was deathly ill and might not live through the transfer to another hospital. His plea fell on deaf ears. He called Freedman's Hospital and talked with J. Mark Cox, a black Adventist physician interning there, who was also barred from Adventist institutions because of his race.[36] He said they had the space at Freedman's and would be happy to help. The Byards traveled by taxi into the District of Columbia, but it was too late. By the time they made it to the hospital, Mrs. Byard had suffered too much. Despite valiant efforts to save her, she died shortly after her arrival.[37]

The death of Lucille Byard became a turning point in the Adventist Church. Although she did not receive healing, her death launched a string of events that eventually led to the healing of many in the African American community. Namely, it was the catalyst for regional conferences that would tend to the needs of African Americans. Of course, this was not what African Americans wanted. They wanted an immediate end to segregation and institutionalized racism in the Seventh-day Adventist Church.

Elder W. G. Turner, the North American Division president, came to pacify the members of the black church in Washington, DC, shortly after Byard's death. He preached the following Saturday morning from 1 Peter 4:12, "Beloved, think it not strange concerning the fiery trial which is to try you, as though some strange thing happened unto you." Turner had scarcely sat down from preaching his sermon before a member rebutted: "Think it not strange? Yes, I think it very strange that there is an Adventist college [Washington Missionary College, now Washington Adventist University] nearby to which I cannot send my children. Yes, I think it is strange! A denominational cafeteria [Review and Herald] in which I cannot be served, and now—this incident. I think it mighty strange! . . . I'm not prepared to hear you say, 'Servants, obey your masters,' meaning the General Conference is our master."[38]

"The Adventist presence in the black population in the United States is two or three times greater than in other ethnic groups."

African Americans were offended that denominational leaders would try to refer to racism and segregation as something they should accept. Blacks were outraged that policies of the church would have them die rather than break racist protocols. They were upset their children could not be educated in the schools of their choice and that many of the policies of the church communicated to African Americans that they were inferior. The black constituency of the Seventh-day Adventist Church had had enough. Regional conferences were neither their desire nor plea, but it became clear that the Seventh-day Adventist Church was simply not willing to integrate, to treat all of its members with love, dignity, and respect as Christ had commanded. Thus, regional conferences became what W. L. Cheatham called the "next best plan."[39]

The birth of regional conferences, although not ideal, did much in the way of providing ministry to African Americans. In a 2008 demographic study by the North American Division of Seventh-day Adventists, the diversity of the Seventh-day Adventist Church was attributed in part to "the success of the regional conferences. The Adventist presence in the black population in the United States is two or three times greater than in other ethnic groups. It is not by

WE, TOO, SING AMERICA

accident that the most visible Seventh-day Adventists in American society are Blacks."[40]

Another benefit of regional conferences is that they have provided leadership positions for blacks in the church. Because of these conferences, African Americans who normally would not be able to sit at the table now have a place. Heretofore, the sentiments of African Americans in the Seventh-day Adventist Church were encapsulated well in Langston Hughes's poem, "I, Too, Sing America":

I, Too, Sing America

I am the darker brother.
They send me to eat in the kitchen
When company comes,
But I laugh,
And eat well,
And grow strong.

Tomorrow,
I'll be at the table
When company comes.
Nobody'll dare
Say to me,
"Eat in the kitchen,"
Then.
Besides,
They'll see how beautiful I am
And be ashamed—

I, too, am America.[41]

As African American Seventh-day Adventist women, we wanted to see our darker brothers have a seat at the table. We worked tirelessly to make it happen. Although African American men are not where they would like to be in the Seventh-day Adventist Church, they are not where they would be in the Seventh-day Adventist Church if African American women did not support and fight for them.

Still, the fight for rights for African Americans in the Seventh-day Adventist Church has been primarily for African American *men*. Seventy years after the inception of regional conferences, most of the representation and leadership has gone to African American men. No one decries the fact that black women have been left in the kitchen. After all, many think that is her place.

Consequently, African American Seventh-day Adventist women have held a peculiar place in history. We have often found ourselves at the intersection of racism and sexism. Being African American and female is what Francis Beale calls a "double jeopardy."[42] It is as if we live and serve in a denomination where "all the women are white and all the Blacks are men."[43] Although there are fights for the rights of women and the rights of African Americans, change and progress for the African American woman has been slow. It seems we have been excluded from both categories. We have seen firsthand what scholars call the "invisibility of black women." This is not a superpower implying literal invisibility but, rather, the fact that black women continue to go unnoticed and unheard.[44]

When the story is told of the women's struggle in the Seventh-day Adventist Church, there is little, if anything, said about the contributions of black women in ministry. In the lists detailing significant women in Adventist history, the names of African American women are strangely absent. I have been to many conferences and meetings on women in ministry in the Seventh-day Adventist Church, and it was not until I was preparing this chapter that I learned of the ministerial contributions of Anna Knight, how her life was threatened because she was a black woman preacher. She had to travel with her Bible *and* her pistol.

When the story is told of the struggle of African Americans in this denomination, we often hear of E. E. Cleveland, who traveled around the globe winning thousands of souls for Christ, but little is said of Celia Cleveland, his wife, who won over three thousand souls for Christ herself.[45] Women like Dr. Lottie Blake, the first black Adventist physician, seldom have their stories told. In 1904, she was the only black female physician with a private practice in Birmingham. Dr. Eva B. Dykes, the first black woman to complete a PhD degree, was also a phenomenal Seventh-day Adventist woman. Mary Stovall broke barriers for African American Adventist women by being the first black and the first female mayor of Hurtsboro, Alabama.

There are others whose stories have gone untold—thousands in the shadows and behind the scenes. From Edgefield Junction, Tennessee, where the first African American Seventh-day Adventist Church was organized in 1886, women who healed were there. Women such as Jennie Allison, who was one of the first black women to join the Seventh-day Adventist Church back in 1883, was one of the charter members of the Edgefield Junction church. There were teachers who taught little black children when no one else would. Bible instructors like Ola Mae Harris and Ida Hanks have worked alongside evangelists for decades, winning souls for Christ. These were, indeed, healers.

Today, we are blessed with trailblazers. Dr. Hyveth Williams was the first black female pastor and the first female senior pastor in the Seventh-day Adventist Church. Dr. Rosa Banks has embodied a long list of firsts: the first female vice president of Oakwood College (now Oakwood University), the first female general field secretary for the North American Division and for the General Conference of Seventh-day Adventists, and the first female associate secretary for the General Conference. She, Dr. Williams, and others like them are healers.

Nevertheless, as African American women in the Seventh-day Adventist Church, we are still in a precarious position—because of both our race and our gender. Our race sometimes puts us out of step with our denomination, and our gender puts us at odds with our race. And nobody decries the fact that we are neither in the dining room with company nor sitting at the table with our darker brother but, rather, serving in both arenas quietly as we always have.

I spoke at a North American Division Fall Council meeting, and afterward, someone came to me and said, "Thank you. Thank you for not being an angry black woman." Being angry is definitely a *warranted* option—but not one that many black women have chosen because we are healers. Maya Angelou said, "You may not control all the events that happen to you, but you can decide not to be reduced by them."[46] Harboring sickness, anger, resentment, and bitterness is debilitating and belittling, to say the least. These negative behaviors inhibit one's ability to bring healing and exhibit one's necessity to receive healing.

There is a healing power that flows from service. When one releases healing, it is returned, pressed down, shaken together, and running over. This is what African American Seventh-day Adventist women have done for well over a century. Looking at their track record of selfless service, I have become convinced that African American women will be great in the kingdom because, for centuries, they have been least of all. But until then:

We laugh,
And eat well,
And grow strong.
Tomorrow,
We'll be at the table
When company comes.
Nobody'll dare
Say to us,
"Eat in the kitchen,"
Then.
Besides,

They'll see how beautiful we are
And be ashamed—
We, too, are America.[47]

Andrea Trusty King, DMin

Dr. Andrea King is an acclaimed international speaker. She is also the author of two books: *Finding Christ* and *The Queen in Me*. She has pastored for over twenty years in Southern California. She is married to her partner in life, love, and service, Dr. Kurt King. Together, they have two children.

Selected Bibliography

Angelou, Maya. *Letter to My Daughter*. Random House, New York, 2008.

Banks, Rosa Taylor. "Sisters in Service." Accessed November 6, 2014. http://www.oakwood.edu/goldmine/hdoc/blacksda/sisters/. Web page discontinued.

Beale, Frances. "Double Jeopardy: To Be Black and Female." In *The Black Woman: An Anthology*, edited by T. Cade. New York: New American Library, 1970.

Benton, Josephine. *Called by God: Stories of Seventh-day Adventist Women Ministers*. Smithsburg, MD: Blackberry Hill Publishers, 1990.

Cleveland, E. E. *Let the Church Roll On: An Autobiography*. Boise, ID: Pacific Press®, 1997.

Clinton, Bill. "Remarks on Presenting the Presidential Citizens Medal," January 8, 2001. Weekly Compilation of Presidential Documents, vol. 37, no. 2 (Monday, January 15, 2001). https://www.govinfo.gov/content/pkg/WCPD-2001-01-15/html/WCPD-2001-01-15-Pg41.htm.

Dykes, James E. "Lifted Lamp in the World's Wild Storm." *Message* magazine, February 1958.

Encyclopedia.com, s.v. "Truth, Sojourner (1797–1883)." Updated May 14, 2018.

http://www.encyclopedia.com/doc/1G2-3437500761.html.

Goldstein, Richard. "Irene Morgan Kirkaldy, 90, Rights Pioneer, Dies." *The New York Times*, August 13, 2007. http://www.nytimes.com/2007/08/13/us/13kirkaldy .html?_r=0.

Haloviak, Bert. "Impact of SDA Eschatological Assumptions on Certain Issues of Social Policy." Paper presented at the Race Relations Summit, Silver Spring, MD, October 27, 1999. http://adventisthistory.wordpress.com/2008/10/26 /lucy-byard/.

Hughes, Langston, and Arna Bontemps, eds. *The Poetry of the Negro, 1746–1970: An Anthology*. Garden City, NY: Doubleday, 1970.

Hull, Gloria, Pat Bell Scott, and Barbara Smith. *All the Women Are White, All the Blacks Are Men, But Some of Us Are Brave*. Old Westbury, NY: Feminist Press, 1982.

Humphrey, Patricia. "Pioneer of Freedom." *Columbia Union Visitor*, February 15, 1989.

Justiss, Jacob. *Angels in Ebony*. Toledo, OH: Jet Printing Service, 1975.

Knight, Anna. *Mississippi Girl*. Nashville, TN: Southern Publishing Association, 1952.

London, Samuel. *Seventh-day Adventists and the Civil Rights Movement*. Jackson, MS: University Press of Mississippi, 2009.

Mabee, Carleton, and Susan Mabee Newhouse. *Sojourner Truth: Slave, Prophet, Legend*. New York: New York University Press, 1995.

Marshall, Norwida A., and R. Steven Norman, eds. *A Star Gives Light: Seventh-day Adventist African-American Heritage; Teacher's Resource Guide*. Decatur, GA: Southern Union Conference of Seventh-day Adventists, 1989.

Morello, Carol. "The Freedom Rider a Nation Nearly Forgot: Woman Who Defied Segregation Finally Gets Her Due." *The Washington Post*, July 30, 2000.

Neufeld, Don, ed. *Seventh-day Adventist Encyclopedia*. Vol. 10 of the Commentary Reference Series. Hagerstown, MD: Review and Herald®, 1976.

Peterson, Frank Loris. *Climbing High Mountains*. Washington, DC: Review and Herald®, 1962.

Reynolds, Louis B. *We Have Tomorrow*. Washington, DC: Review and Herald®, 1984.

Sahlin, Monte, and Paul Richardson. *Seventh-day Adventists in North America—A Demographic Profile*. North American Division Secretariat Demographic Survey. Milton Freewater, OR: Center for Creative Ministry, 2008.

Schwartz, R. W. *Light Bearers to the Remnant*. Mountain View, CA: Pacific Press®, 1979.

Sepulveda, Ciro, Tia Graves, and Dejuan Knight. "Anna Knight." In *Ladies of Oakwood*. Huntsville, AL: Oakwood College Press, 2003.

Sesko, Amanda, and Monica Biernat. "Prototypes of Race and Gender: The Invisibility of Black Women." *Journal of Experimental Social Psychology* 46, no. 2 (2010): 357.

Singleton, Harold. "Vanguard of Torchbearers: The Story of Anna Knight." *North*

American Informant, March/April 1968.

Stanton, Elizabeth Cady, Susan B. Anthony, and Matilda J. Gage, eds. *History of Woman Suffrage*. Vol. 1. Rochester, NY: Susan B. Anthony, Charles Mann, 1881.

"Story of Anna Knight, as told to A. W. Spalding in Atlanta, Georgia, Nov. 19, 22, 1914." Ellen G. White Estate file DF 372-1, 1914.

Truth, Sojourner. "Ain't I a Woman?" Speech given at the Women's Convention, Akron, Ohio, May 28, 29, 1851.

Truth, Sojourner. *The Narrative of Sojourner Truth*. Dictated by Sojourner Truth. Edited by Olive Gilbert. Boston: self-pub., 1850.

Tuck, Stephen G. N. *We Ain't What We Ought to Be: The Black Freedom Struggle From Emancipation to Obama*. Cambridge, MA: Belknap Press, 2010.

Yearbook of the Seventh-Day Adventist Denomination. Washington, DC: Review and Herald®, 1941.

You Don't Have to Ride Jim Crow! Public Television's Documentary of the 1947 Journey of Reconciliation, America's First Freedom Ride. Film produced by Robin Washington for Corporation for Public Broadcasting, 2007.

---

1. Don F. Neufeld, ed., *Seventh-day Adventist Encyclopedia*, vol. 10 of the Commentary Reference Series (Hagerstown, MD: Review and Herald®, 1976), s.v. "Byington, John."

2. Neufeld, s.v. "Kellogg, John Preston"; James L. Hayward, "Kellogg, John Harvey (1852–1943)", Encyclopedia of Seventh-day Adventists, accessed August 31, 2021, https://encyclopedia.adventist.org/article?id=89LQ.

3. James E. Dykes, "Lifted Lamp in the World's Wild Storm," *Message* magazine, February 1958, 27.

4. Carleton Mabee and Susan Mabee Newhouse, *Sojourner Truth: Slave, Prophet, Legend* (New York: New York University Press, 1995), 13.

5. Encyclopedia.com, s.v. "Truth, Sojourner" (1797–1883)," last modified May 14, 2018, http://www.encyclopedia.com/doc/1G2-3437500761.html.

6. Frank Loris Peterson, *Climbing High Mountains* (Washington, DC: Review and Herald®, 1962), 29.

7. Mabee and Newhouse, *Sojourner Truth*, 83.

8. Peterson, *Climbing High Mountains*, 33.

9. Sojourner Truth, *The Narrative of Sojourner Truth*, ed. Olive Gilbert (Boston: The Author, 1850), 110.

10. Patricia Humphrey, "Pioneer of Freedom," *Columbia Union Visitor*, February 15, 1989, 4.

11. Elizabeth Cady Stanton, Susan B. Anthony, and Matilda Joslyn Gage, eds., *History of Woman Suffrage*, vol. 1 (Rochester, NY: Susan B. Anthony, Charles Mann, 1881), 115.

12. Stanton, Anthony, and Gage, 115.

13. Stanton, Anthony, and Gage, 115.

14. Stanton, Anthony, and Gage, 115.

15. Sojourner Truth, "Ain't I a Woman?" Women's Convention, Akron, Ohio, May 28, 29, 1851.

16. Truth.

17. Rosa Taylor Banks, "Sisters in Service," accessed November 6, 2014, http://www

AFRICAN AMERICAN SEVENTH-DAY ADVENTIST HEALERS IN A MULTICULTURAL NATION

.oakwood.edu/goldmine/hdoc/blacksda/sisters/ (page discontinued).

18. Ciro Sepulveda, Tia Graves, and Dejuan Knight, "Anna Knight," in *Ladies of Oakwood* (Huntsville, AL: Oakwood College Press, 2003), 17.

19. Sepulveda, Graves, and Knight, 22.

20. Sepulveda, Graves, and Knight, 24.

21. Anna Knight, *Mississippi Girl* (Nashville, TN: Southern Publishing Association, 1952), 160.

22. "Story of Anna Knight, as told to A. W. Spalding in Atlanta, Georgia, Nov. 19, 22, 1914" (Ellen G. White Estate file DF 372-1, 1914), 11.

23. "Story of Anna Knight," 13.

24. Knight, *Mississippi Girl*, 167.

25. Harold Singleton, "Vanguard of Torchbearers: The Story of Anna Knight," *North American Informant*, March/April 1968, 1.

26. *Yearbook of the Seventh-Day Adventist Denomination* (Washington, DC: Review and Herald®, 1941), 64.

27. Josephine Benton, *Called by God: Stories of Seventh-day Adventist Women Ministers* (Smithsburg, MD: Blackberry Hill Publishers, 1990), 101.

28. "Story of Anna Knight," 9.

29. Knight, *Mississippi Girl*, 223.

30. *You Don't Have to Ride Jim Crow! Public Television's Documentary of the 1947 Journey of Reconciliation, America's First Freedom Ride.* Film produced by Robin Washington for Corporation for Public Broadcasting, 2007.

31. Carol Morello, "The Freedom Rider a Nation Nearly Forgot: Woman Who Defied Segregation Finally Gets Her Due," *The Washington Post*, July 30, 2000, https://www.washington post.com/archive/politics/2000/07/30/the-freedom-rider-a-nation-nearly-forgot/f4568 ccf-ae89-47c7-9c53-ba2d2ea70da5/.

32. Stephen G. N. Tuck, *We Ain't What We Ought to Be: The Black Freedom Struggle From Emancipation to Obama* (Cambridge, MA: Belknap Press, 2010), 237.

33. Bill Clinton, "Remarks on Presenting the Presidential Citizens Medal," January 8, 2001, Weekly Compilation of Presidential Documents, vol. 37, no. 2 (Monday, January 15, 2001), 41–49, https://www.govinfo.gov/content/pkg/WCPD-2001-01-15/html /WCPD-2001-01-15-Pg41.htm.

34. Richard Goldstein, "Irene Morgan Kirkaldy, 90, Rights Pioneer, Dies," *The New York Times*, August 13, 2007, http://www.nytimes.com/2007/08/13/us/13kirkaldy.html?_r=0.

35. Samuel London, *Seventh-day Adventists and the Civil Rights Movement* (Jackson: University Press of Mississippi, 2009), 142.

36. London, 144.

37. R. W. Schwartz, *Light Bearers to the Remnant* (Mountain View, CA: Pacific Press®, 1979), 566.

38. Jacob Justiss, *Angels in Ebony* (Toledo, OH: Jet Printing Service, 1975), 43, 44.

39. Bert Haloviak, "Impact of SDA Eschatological Assumptions on Certain Issues of Social Policy" (Race Summit Workshop Presentation, October 27, 1999), http://adventist history.wordpress.com/2008/10/26/lucy-byard/.

40. Monte Sahlin and Paul Richardson, *Seventh-day Adventists in North America—A Demographic Profile: North American Division Secretariat Demographic Survey* (Milton Freewater, OR: Center for Creative Ministry, 2008), 14

41. Langston Hughes and Arna Bontemps, eds., *The Poetry of the Negro, 1746–1970: An Anthology* (Garden City, NY: Doubleday, 1970), 182.

66

42. Frances Beale, "Double Jeopardy: To Be Black and Female," in *The Black Woman: An Anthology*, ed. T. Cade (New York: New American Library, 1970), 90–100.

43. This phrase is borrowed from the book edited by Gloria Hull, Pat Bell Scott, and Barbara Smith, *All the Women Are White, All the Blacks Are Men, but Some of Us Are Brave* (Old Westbury, NY: Feminist Press, 1982).

44. Amanda Sesko and Monica Biernat, "Prototypes of Race and Gender: The Invisibility of Black Women," *Journal of Experimental Social Psychology* 46, no. 2 (2010): 357.

45. Norwida A. Marshal and R. Steven Norman, eds., *A Star Gives Light: Seventh-day Adventist African-American Heritage; Teacher's Resource Guide* (Decatur, GA: Southern Union Conference of Seventh-day Adventists, 1989), 167.

46. Maya Angelou, *Letter to My Daughter* (Random House, New York, 2008), xii.

47. Hughes and Bontemps, *Poetry of the Negro*, 182.

ANTHONY PASCHAL

Westward Leading

Healing Western Style: The African Diaspora
Arrives in Compromised California Healing in a Free State

G o West Young Man, Go West."[1] In the mid-1800s, there was a popular movement to California. The excitement became known as the gold rush. Everyone was rushing to California, including fugitive slaves who had not been set free but who understood they could make a detour on the Underground Railroad and go where the gold was. Not much is written about black people on that journey.

For California to become a state and enter the Union, it had to make an agreement that it would be a free state but fugitive slaves would be returned to the plantations. The state would receive money for its commitment to the understanding. As the climate began to change, it was discovered that blacks, too, had migrated to and settled on the West Coast. In fact, the farther west one went, the more the strategy to address African American issues changed. California was a free state, and for Seventh-day Adventists, how to enhance the black work became a priority. In the climate of the state, it seemed safe to begin outreach work in the area of health.

In the early 1900s, an Adventist medical missionary woman by the name of Jeannie Ireland came to the area known today as Watts, California. Approximately six thousand blacks were in the area, which became a safe place for blacks to settle upon their arrival to California.

Ireland began to hold Bible studies in this community in the home of Theodore Troy. He and his older brother would become synonymous with West Coast black Adventism. Troy willingly opened up his home, where Ireland also taught hygiene and special medical treatments for two years. In 1908, the first black church west of Kansas City was formed with twenty-eight members. This core of individuals made stellar contributions to the Seventh-day Adventist cause and the wider society. Troy's son, Owen, built on the health and Bible studies modeled by Ireland and went on to become a pastor, evangelist, radio broadcaster, musician, scholar, and administrator. With numbers still small yet growing, wearing many hats was business as usual. Those who became black leaders in the church were well respected. Owen's wife, Ruby, and her brother, Aaron, were the children of a former jazz musician and a brick mason from Louisiana, Paul Bontemps, and his wife, Maria. Paul constructed a lot of Adventist church buildings in California. He soon entered the ministry and built congregations. Aaron became a celebrated author and was one of the leading figures in the Harlem Renaissance.

Ruth Temple became the first female physician in Los Angeles and a noted pioneer of public health measures for the city's neediest classes.

In his book *Lewis C. Sheafe: Apostle to Black America,*[2] author Douglas Morgan states that Sheafe arrived in California on January 30, 1915, to pastor the new Berean Seventh-day Adventist Church. There is a Berean Seventh-day Adventist Church in Los Angeles today. It was formed in 1939 and probably is not the same Berean Seventh-day Adventist Church that was established in 1915. It became clear to Sheafe that the further west one came, the easier it appeared to address issues of racial concern among Seventh-day Adventists. However, he discovered that integration doesn't erase racial attitudes. In one discussion, the early black leadership and members had an issue with Ellen White's statement emphatically warning blacks not to address the racial issue. They were admonished to remain silent, so to speak. The statement also added that black leadership simply should not consider themselves equal with white leadership. There was no need to fight for positions of administrative leadership. Lewis Sheafe and company became disturbed by the position of white leadership and that these brothers in Christ would take such a stand in a territory presented as an integrated field. This would certainly be a model of heavenly unity where all races would be treated as equals. They saw this stance, perhaps mistakenly so, as unmovable and felt that it had become a doctrine of the church. The small but strong group wanted the Southern California Conference to denounce this position.

Appeals were made, and for whatever the reasons were at that time, the Southern California Conference would not denounce those statements as an official view of the Seventh-day Adventist Church. So, in one of the wonderfully exciting business meetings of the Berean Church of that era, it was voted to leave the Southern California Conference. The congregation did not agree with the stance of leadership. According to them, the position was not in line with the Bible. They left the denomination as a congregation.

It would be interesting to research the history of what actually happened. What was the process for a hearing? How did the deciding committee view the issue as part of a state culture that had come about as a compromise regarding being a slave state or a free state? After all, to be a part of a system that was to return fugitive enslaved persons to their plantations as part of an agreement to be a free state may seem paradoxical on the one hand and an oxymoron on the fingers of the same hand! What was it like to be in the room where it all happened? Being a "free" state apparently didn't apply to all citizens. Does the church merely reflect the social climate, or is it an army set up by divine appointment to tear down walls of racial divide?

Today, there is a Berean Church (located at 12th and Adams Boulevard in Los Angeles) that eventually came back into the denomination in the 1930s and appears to be committed to keeping the dream alive. Perhaps the DNA of the original church is still prominent as many consider it a church that speaks strongly on issues that affect its progress.

The early days of West Coast Adventist leadership and healers laid a foundation for many black leaders to come. Other notable people would follow Dr. Ruth Temple and begin making a tremendous impact in California. At that time, it seemed that the way into ministry was through the medical missionary approach.

Dennis T. Black, an architect, a musician, and a pastor in good stead, designed part of the 31st Street Church building. He owned a junkyard and had plenty of money. I interviewed him one day, and he stated that he didn't need to become a pastor to get money; he already had plenty of it. He was assigned to pastor the still-infant Berean Church, which he led for seventeen years. He blessed me as a baby, baptized me, and performed my marriage ceremony. He was a gifted architect who eventually designed the building and led the Berean Church members in building the structure that is used for worship to this day. His view was that the members should buy the property for their church building (not waiting for conference approval and a vote) and deed it over to the conference. I suppose he believed that people of color could engage in community raising of funds and purchase property they could control.

> The early days of West Coast Adventist leadership and healers laid a foundation for many black leaders to come.

He once shared a story of running out of money to help purchase the property for the Berean Church. He envisioned expansion and saw a need to buy the remaining lots to the end of the block. After he

71

asked for assistance from the conference to realize the dream, the administrative leaders (integrated, but perhaps not yet equal) said to him, "You people don't need that much land." If you attend the Berean Church today, you may experience frustration in your search for adequate parking. To many, the struggle remains when their fate is left to those who may not address their ability to pay expenses but choose to exercise selective power to decide whether they are warranted to have what they are lawfully asking for.

Other names of note include G. N. Banks, Lorenzo Paytee, and Dr. David Taylor. Dr. Taylor became a model leader in youth ministry. He has been instrumental in developing and cultivating many young people into strong leaders in the church. He was a regular speaker for Youth Weeks of Prayer. He has been a stalwart pastor, administrator, and professor in the Seventh-day Adventist Church.

Many others are worthy of special notice for major contributions on the West Coast of the United States. Elder Canson, Major White, R. W. Nelson, and Anita Mackey are all key individuals who helped build on the foundation of the Bontemps and Dr. Ruth Temple— pioneers of the Seventh-day Adventist work in California. These and many more have enhanced the work of black Adventists in the West. On March 9, 2013, a Lorenzo Paytee Golf Classic began on a historic weekend at Los Angeles Adventist Academy. That institution opened its doors in 1923 and began to educate blacks. Among the students who attended and affected the world church were Dr. Calvin B. Rock, former president of Oakwood University and vice president of the General Conference of Seventh-day Adventists; E. C. Ward, pastor elite of the San Diego 31st Street Church, the Los Angeles Berean Church, and the Oakwood University Church in Huntsville, Alabama. Their wives and other leaders have also come out of that Los Angeles Academy experience. In 2013, it celebrated ninety years of effective education. In Los Angeles, the 31st Street Church, the University Seventh day Adventist Church, the Market Street Church, and the Berean Church all stand as historical centers of black leadership and development.

As we consider the future, social norms on the West Coast, particularly in California as a free state in a broader sense of the term, will become more inclusive. The Seventh-day Adventist Church will have to move beyond surface jargon and practice to an authentic arena where equality can be modeled. For several decades, the West Coast has considered itself a model of integration and unity for the church. What that means in certain circles is that those who grew up on the West Coast often see themselves as knowing how to talk and mesh with our white brothers and sisters to get some things accomplished—sometimes arrogantly assuming they do so more effectively than blacks in other parts of the United States. That view can probably be debated on a large scale, but that posture can be credited with results, along with thanks to schools such as Pacific Union College, where many of our West Coast members attended and rubbed shoulders with other races and became leaders of the church. Although this may be true in certain circles, it raises concerns for many as to whether the voice and the posture for activism in addressing racial issues are fearless and will lead to a distinct difference regarding the interests of black members.

Knowing our history as contributors to the building up of the work is crucial for strengthening our position as a people to be heard and respected. I've heard Dr. Michelle Alexander make the statement, "If a people don't know their history, they will soon be history." So what stands consistently noted is that with the seasons of the Underground Railroad to freedom, the Emancipation Proclamation, the Reconstruction period, Black Renaissance, Black Wall Street, and urban challenges throughout our nation today—together with challenges within Seventh-day Adventism regarding structure, education, community health, and more, there is a constant climate that has caused, and in many cases driven, black people to come together, engage in serious dialogue, create a strategy, and develop a collective agenda.

Today, the black church, particularly on the West Coast (and perhaps all over), faces homelessness, within both its membership and its community; joblessness, both within its membership and its community; hunger; and a high number of blacks in the prison population. Dr. Michelle Alexander, in her book *The New Jim Crow*, points out that today, more blacks are connected to the prison system—either on parole, serving time, or involved in the court system—than were enslaved in 1850.[3] An agenda has been set before us. We still have a lot of work to do, even as a prophetic church of African descendants on the West Coast.

Anthony Paschal

Born in Memphis, Tennessee, and raised in Compton, California, Anthony enjoyed early education in the Seventh-day Adventist schools Los Angeles Union Elementary and Lynwood Academy. He is a graduate of Oakwood University in Huntsville, Alabama, and Andrews University's Seventh-day Adventist Theological Seminary in Berrien Springs, Michigan. He has served as a pastor in Los Angeles, California, and Riverside, California. He also served for a short stint as vice president in the Southeastern California Conference.

1. J. W. Ellison, s.v. " 'Go West, Young Man, Go West,' " Encyclopedia.com, https://www.encyclopedia.com/history/dictionaries-thesauruses-pictures-and-press-releases/go-west-young-man-go-west.

2. Douglas Morgan, *Lewis C. Sheafe: Apostle to Black America* (Hagerstown, MD: Review and Herald®, 2010).

3. Michelle Alexander, *The New Jim Crow: Mass Incarceration in the Age of Colorblindness* (New York: New Press, 2010).

JAMES L. KYLE

To Dream, to Be, to Act:
Healing a Sick Society

D espite all the scientific breakthroughs and the ever-increasing
cost of health care in America, we still rank near the middle
of developed countries in life expectancy. We pay more than any
other people on the planet for health care; but, clearly, we aren't
getting our money's worth. Our society is still beleaguered with the
excessive burden of chronic disease. Some estimate that one out of
every two Americans is overweight or obese. Diabetes is an epidemic
in this country, and health disparities among minority populations
are hardly even recognized—let alone addressed. While our nation
debates the merits of legalizing marijuana, needless thousands die
on our nation's highways from accidents caused by the legal drug,
alcohol. It is to this battleground that today's physician is called to
respond.

To heal our society will be a tall order. What type of physician will
it take to meet this challenge?

There are some who look at the life of a physician and assume that he
or she lives a charmed existence with minimal stress, high pay, and great
personal satisfaction. While I love what I do, it has certainly been no
picnic to get where I am today. But rather than discuss my unusual journey, it would be more advantageous to reflect on our collective journey.

The journey of anyone dedicated to the healing of others starts with a dream. The dreamer is not one who remains asleep but one who, with eyes wide open, sees and empathizes with the plight of the human race and longs to make a difference. That dream is amplified by, and often the direct result of, God's call on the life. When this happens, a dream is more than wishful thinking. It becomes a living purpose, a fire in the bones that cannot be quenched by anything but active engagement in the pursuit of that calling. I was already an ordained minister of the gospel when I sensed God's calling on my life to expand my work into medicine. I was initially uncertain of how I would begin or whether this was truly God's call.

When I shared the notion of returning to school to complete my premed studies and to eventually apply to medical school, many of my associates thought I had lost my mind. I was thirty years old, and many thought that I was just too old to ever get into medical school. Others questioned my motives as self-serving, greedy, or being driven by blind ambition. I was accused of "leaving the work" and of succumbing to avarice and now worshiping mammon.

For some time, I felt like an outcast from my ministerial colleagues, and this cost me dearly in my spiritual life. The dream became a painful and heavy burden. I was preached about and became the hidden subject of church publications regarding faithfulness or the lack of it. When I took my leave of absence from the Breath of Life ministry, I got a feeler from a conference to lead out in the work but was later told that no formal call would be coming because there was a concern that I would set a bad example for the young ministers, who themselves might seek to pursue an alternate career path.

For many would-be healers, those seeking to make a difference in the world, there is always a high cost to be paid for daring to dream or having the audacity to share those dreams with others. You recall the price Joseph paid for sharing his dream with his family. He was the object of jealousy, hatred, and a murder conspiracy. He was captured, sold into slavery, falsely accused, and imprisoned. Dreaming sometimes comes at a considerable cost. But the price of living a dreamless life is much higher. The dreamless wander aimlessly through life seeking the paths of least resistance and living lives that fall far short of God's expectations. One need not aspire to medicine to be considered a dreamer. But whatever your aspiration, to live without a dream is to drink deeply from the cup of mediocrity, and when you have had your fill, your mind will be too dulled to even know what you could have been.

> Dreaming sometimes comes at a considerable cost. But the price of living a dreamless life is much higher.

I dreamed of connecting the right arm of the gospel to the ministry of the church. Somewhere along the way, the right arm had become amputated and relegated to some suspicious status of secondary significance. Adventist physicians were most valuable to the church because of their tithe-paying potential and the occasional health minute in an evangelistic crusade. We were always valued in foreign missions but of limited use domestically. Some clergy members saw physicians as want-to-be preachers and would shun having them in positions of church leadership. Fortunately, this climate has improved, but with the issues that still plague our inner cities, there is an even greater need for creative intervention to affect the many troubled and hopeless lives.

Given the extremes of affluence and poverty in America, physicians are needed to deliver care to many for whom access to primary and specialty care has been out of reach. The political-ideological divide over the Affordable Care Act has caused many governors to refuse to expand their Medicaid programs in protest. This has kept millions of poor people from obtaining needed medical coverage. By and large, the American health-care industry has failed to respond to the Institute of Medicine report on health-care disparities and the unequal treatment that minorities in this country experience daily.

For dreamers, those looking to make a difference, there are still mountains to climb and valleys to cross. Justice and equity in health care remain elusive.

Not only are healers called to dream, but the dreamer must become the fulfillment of his or her intent. In other words, dreamers cannot be content to sleep away their desired future. We must *be* the dream; we must live it without surrender or equivocation. Our treatment of patients must reflect a standard of care that strives for excellence, compassion, and efficiency. The personal development of the healer is not just in clinical knowledge; it is also in the development of the intellect and the soul. Medicine is in desperate need of men and women of integrity, empathy, and courage. We must become all that God and our profession beckon us to be.

I have been in countless meetings and circumstances where some have failed to live up to their high calling when challenged to stand for principle, to shun avarice or bigotry. Fortunately, I have also seen so many physicians live with honor, dignity, and compassion that I am encouraged for the future of my profession. Physicians are privileged to be in positions of trust to treat those who suffer from devastating illness and hopelessness. No profession affords such an opportunity to walk life's difficult journey with the vulnerable and perishing. The physician greets young lives as they come into the world and holds the hands of those soon to exit this life. Physicians have the opportunity to stamp out disease, prevent illnesses, and bring healing and cure to so many.

But physicians must be what they call their patients to become. Their lifestyles must be free of the health-destroying habits they call their patients to shun. If I never exercise, then why should my patients? Patients want to see their doctor *do* as well as *say*. It is time for the healers to heal themselves first.

A September 2010 study done by the University of Michigan health system concluded that physicians' confidence in their ability to counsel patients on a healthy diet and exercise may be related to their own personal habits. The authors went on to say that factors that predicted confidence in counseling included the doctor's own exercise time, whether the doctor was overweight, and whether the doctor had adequate training in counseling patients.[1]

Another study demonstrated that a physician's personal lifestyle habits and attitude toward lifestyle counseling determine the effectiveness of their efforts.

"We examined the relation of physicians' clinical specialty, personal health habits, and health-related beliefs to their practices in counseling about smoking, weight, exercise, and alcohol. We surveyed a random sample of members of a county medical society in selected specialties. Physicians with better personal health habits and more positive attitudes toward counseling counsel a broader range of patients and counsel more aggressively. Surgeons counsel less than nonsurgeons, even after controlling for differences in health-related attitudes and personal habits."[2]

To be or not to be. That is still the question. No, physicians are not perfect, nor are they superhuman. They don't have to look like Olympic athletes in order to have credible standing as they work with patients. They, too, are subject to disease and death. No one would reasonably assume otherwise. But a physician has an opportunity to adopt a lifestyle that can inspire and encourage their patients to live better and healthier. And if we can motivate them to adopt healthier lifestyles, we can begin to decrease the burden of chronic disease that now plagues our country. Patients would probably be more impressed with their doctor's imperfect attempts at a healthy lifestyle than they would be with a verbal exhortation accompanied by no effort at all.

Finally, the physician must also act. No dream is worthy unless the dreamer is willing to act upon it. Action speaks; words only whisper.

The American health system is in dire need of physicians willing to confront the inequities of health disparities and the intrusions of the corporate food industry into the lives of their patients. The US food industry has conspired to create unhealthy foods for profit.

Michael Moss, in his book, *Salt, Sugar, Fat*, shared this insight regarding the American food industry: The food industry has meticulously calculated what is known as the " 'bliss point' or the precise amount of sugar or fat or salt that will send consumers over the moon." They conspire and scientifically calculate how to make processed foods addictive.[3]

Physicians have an obligation not only to provide the best medical care they can but also to spotlight the societal threats to the very patients they are treating. If indeed the food industry has conspired to make America fat for the benefit of its profits, then to be silent makes us complicit. Physicians have the opportunity to use their education, skills, and voices to inform their patients and the community at large how they can live longer and better. Given the significant health-care disparities facing minority communities, many of which have still not been formally addressed by the American health-care establishment, we must not settle for simply treating disease. We must work to empower communities and individuals to prevent disease and live healthy lives. For me, that is also part of the dream. That is my calling. Through research, treatment, and advocacy, physicians are the guardians of the desperate and hopeless. To dream, to be, to act. What a privilege to be called a healer!

James L. Kyle

Dr. Kyle is currently the Medical Director for Quality, Diversity, Equity & Inclusion at LA CARE, the nation's largest public health plan. He is also the current senior pastor of the Vallejo Drive Seventh-day Adventist Church in Glendale, California. Previously he served as the dean of the Loma Linda University School of Public Health.

1. Michael Howe et al., "Patient Related Diet and Exercise Counseling: Do Providers' Own Lifestyle Habits Matter?" *Preventive Cardiology* 13, no. 4 (2010), https://doi.org/10.1111/j.1751-7141.2010.00079.x.

2. Kenneth B. Wells et al., "Do Physicians Preach What They Practice? A Study of Physicians' Health Habits and Counseling Practices," abstract, *JAMA* 252, no. 20, https://doi.org/10.1001/jama.252.20.2846.

3. Michael Moss, *Salt, Sugar, Fat: How the Food Giants Hooked Us* (New York: Random House, 2013), xxv, 347.

MAURY JACKSON

Healing Shepherds and the Pastoral Care of African American Religioracial Ills

P astors and medical practitioners work under overlapping assumptions and norms. It is often said of, and by, physicians that they "practice" medicine. The key word, of course, is *practice*. Clergy, who like to think of themselves as physicians of the soul, also "practice" ministry.[1] Describing the healing arts as a "practice" suggests that medical and clerical practitioners know the limits of their healing crafts. In medicine, however, the term *practice* has at times been used by physicians as an excuse to blur the lines between medical treatments that serve therapeutic purposes and those that serve the purposes of nontherapeutic research. People of African descent know well this side of the horrors that resulted from Western medical practice. This has induced an understandable fear, on their part, of those who practice the healing arts. The technical term for this fear is *iatrophobia*.[2] Iatrophobia occurs when a sick person fears the cure of the healer more than the illness from which he suffers.

While African American people feared physicians who, in the name of healing their bodies, were really subjecting them to research,

Portions of this chapter were previously published on the *Adventist Today* website October 21, 2018, and in the journal *Cultural and Religious Studies*, vol. 7, no. 9, September 2019. The chapter extends and expands on the ideas articulated in these earlier forms.

they should fear pastoral practitioners for the opposite reason. When pastors profess to be the spiritual healers of a people and yet fail to take their context of ministry as not only a place to offer service but also as the location for research into the workings of God among people today, they ought to be distrusted. Too often, African American clergy members (Adventist and non-Adventist) embrace the theological training handed down to them by white systematic theologians without questioning whether or not it rings true to their context; that is, does it "apply" to their practices of healing sociospiritual ills. This model of ministry is seen as applied theology. It is a top-down theology. Systematic theologians manufacture the theological propositions, and the pastors "apply" them in their context of ministry. This model assumes that theology is done in some armchair among biblical and historical scholars of religion and is then applied by clergy on the ground. On the contrary, practical theology is a bottom-up theology. It is theological care and research done at the same time. This model assumes that God is still working among His people and that pastoral healers can discover His continuing revelation in the practice of their ministries. When this happens, "the social and political life of black people can be transformed by bridging the gap between black theology and the ministry of the black church."[3] Pastors who practice in this way can reflect on and revise their practices in light of what they learn about the ways of God as understood in community.[4]

Black theology is practical theology, and when African American clerics attempt to offer a healing word, it should not be one that begins in a context different from that of those to whom they seek to minister or one that does not take seriously the lived experience of black people. To practice ministry in this way is to bring about a justifiable fear of the spiritual healer. I'm reminded of Jesus' words in Nazareth recorded by the physician Luke. Jesus said, "No doubt you will quote this proverb to Me, 'Physician, heal yourself!' " (Luke 4:23,

NASB). Healing begins at home. Our foremothers and forefathers took seriously the task of being the agents of their own healing. After all, when the medical profession aided the institution of slavery, the white healing practitioner was not to be trusted. Black people began their healing process in the daytime and nighttime dreams of those persons deeply immersed in slave religion. As Jon Michael Spencer writes, "Since dreams are the compensatory, prophetic, and therapeutic guides to transformation, health and wholeness, the slaves needed dreams—day dreams and night dreams and the dreams of their spirituals—to heal their many wounds."[5] Our foreparents were the physicians who healed themselves—or at least started the self-healing process.

We need to continue it today. The need for religioracial healing among African American people calls for the African American Adventist pastor-healer to (1) employ black theology as the conceptual framework for applying caring techniques, (2) reclaim the Bible as the primary source for nurturing social solidarity, and (3) replot the pan-African narrative in ways that give voice to a subversive memory of resistance. In this essay, I will begin by clarifying some ways in which I understand the concepts that relate to race and religion in contemporary thought. The second part examines the way African Americans employ black theology, pan-African studies, and the Bible to construct a normative theology. The final part discusses why all of this has become a necessary resource for African American Adventist pastors as healing shepherds.

Critical race theory and the broken symbol of "blackness"

I feel the need to begin by offering two clarifying comments. These comments are in the form of assertions regarding racial identity that I now take as a given since the emergence of critical race theory.[6] Critical race theory has challenged the ordinary concept of race and taught us to think more critically about the function of racial discourse. The first claim that I have come to accept as true is that there is no biological entity known as "a race of people." We have no markers that determine one race from another: not genotype, not phenotype, and not complexion.[7] The concept of race is purely a social construction like that of football games, basketball scores, and political elections.[8] Race is a concept that is not rooted in any truth about biology. Its truth is in sociology, which has come to expose the biological myth that undergirds racial discourse.

The second claim that I have come to accept is that, for me, to speak of a "black" race or to write about "black theology" is to recognize the term as a broken symbol that tries to recapture and recover the glorious story of an identifiable people. I call this symbol "broken" because it roughly helps to recapture the story of an identifiable people, but it does so by employing the myth of race to hold the narrative in place. At this point, it might be helpful to note that myth is not inherently evil.[9] It serves as an interpretative activity "addressed to questions of origin, of moral ambiguity, of the meaning of suffering and death, and of anomalous phenomena that cannot be assimilated to existing conceptual systems."[10] People of African descent in America have used the myth of a "black" racial identity to perform all of the tasks listed here by Wayne Proudfoot. The broken symbol "black" helped people of African descent to address questions of origin, moral ambiguity, meaningless suffering, and the anomalies of their living conditions.

So then, we may stipulate that the term *black* throughout this essay signifies a modern people whose contingent origins and historical connection with Africa presents a peculiar problem in modern, Western history. I say "stipulate" because the ordinary person has learned to use the concept of race in ways that often fail to employ the term as a socially constructed category. When we take note of the social construction of race, we are able to see with Paul Harvey that "a complex of historical factors (such as the gigantic global enterprise of the African slave trade) and mythic groundings (such as stories from the Old Testament) influenced the construction of modern racial categories."[11]

Replotting the pan-African story
to give voice to subversive memories of resistance

It is important to review this history not only in light of the "mis-education *of* the Negro"[12] but also, more so, in light of the mis-education *about* the Negro.

With respect to the origins of African people in this hemisphere, this story is still being contested among African American scholars. African American people learned to retell their stories in ways that were empowering to the members of the community. One of the ways of telling their story was to begin beyond the eastern coastline of the Western Hemisphere. Historian Lerone Bennett Jr., while acknowledging the possibility of pre-Columbian African contact with the new world, nevertheless chooses to identify the month of August (in the year 1619) as the date that initiated the real start of African America.[13] This date is significant, yet many scholars in the discipline of black studies contest the notion that Africans first encountered the Atlantic shores only after Columbus and the European explorers. These scholars search for hints of African exploration in the Western Hemisphere. Scholars like Ivan Van Sertima have demonstrated through well-reasoned arguments (based on indigenous Amerindian oral tradition, linguistic studies, textual documents, and cultural artifacts) that evidence of an African presence in pre-Columbian America cannot be ignored.[14] While this is not the forum in which to go into the details of his argument, it must be acknowledged that scholars can no longer dismiss the evidence upon which those types of arguments are based.

Not only is the question of where to begin the origins of African peoples in the Western Hemisphere under dispute among African

American scholars, but so, too, is the question of how much of a role European spirituality played in the formation of the African religious consciousness. The answer to this question can be decisive for religious practitioners who offer religioracial healing for African American people. Once again, the work of pan-African scholars such as Cheikh Anta Diop and W. E. B. Dubois and Americana scholars such as Albert J. Raboteau exhibit how Africa's gift to the world of human culture is a sophisticated religious sensibility and understanding.[15] This was true of early African Christians, whether Athanasius, Tertullian, Origen, or Augustine.[16] African people were the major fathers shaping the Christian church during the patristic period. However true this was of early African Christian theological thinkers, it was also true of early non-Christian African theology. Arguably, the first documented monotheist in human history was the African monarch Akhenaton.[17] Moreover, what was true regarding the sophistication of early African Christian and non-Christian theology is also true of African theological thinking during the early post-Medieval period. Africans did not have a primitive animistic theology of nature worship, as has been taught for so long. According to religious historian Henry Mitchell, African traditional religion is more accurately described as bureaucratic monotheism.[18]

This view of divine reality imagines the spiritual energy of heaven scattered among various agents, yet at the same time, it imagines an exalted God as the Most-High spiritual Entity. The sophisticated African religious mind recognized the omnipresent divine spirit. The notion that God's spirit permeates all places influenced the thinking of those captives who made up "the greatest migration in recorded history."[19] It was because African religious consciousness was open to the divine spirit (in *all* places and *all* people) that the first encounters the Africans had with the Bible brought complex responses. God's presence is everywhere, and this view allowed Africa's children to receive the Bible as an object of reverence.[20] However (because of the African openness to the divine presence in *all* things and places), unlike their European counterparts, Africa's children did not restrict their theological resources to revelation in a book.[21] The captives in the New World did realize, however, that as a people with few material resources, this Text was an indispensable resource for cultural competency (not to mention human spirituality).

Our broken symbols can become the source of healing for others.

History documents the transatlantic slave trade and those people of African descent who became the focal point of bondage in America. So the meaning of suffering and death became central to African captives. The dark complexion of a minority African people in a majority European colony signaled to them that "there was no hiding place" over here. Like it or not, Negro people, colored people, black people, or African Americans comprised the social group who suffered oppression on the basis of a socially constructed racial identity of being "black." If we accept the identity of African Americans not to biologically describe a racial group but as a cultural description of a people with a precious heritage, then we have a starting point for defining the raciated social group.

So then, this broken symbol of "black people" is helpful for keeping the mission of African American people grounded. I want us to think about more than black theology or African American Adventists in general. But to think more specifically about the healing shepherds among them, I need to clarify what it means to be a healer while at the same time being a human—you are a wounded healer (see Luke 4:23). Henri Nouwen notes that "in our own woundedness we can become a source of life for others."[22] Our broken symbols can become the source of healing for others.

So in discussing African American Adventist healers in a multi-cultural nation, I want to turn the surgical knife toward my own generation of black Adventist theologians.[23] James Cone writes about Malcolm X and his critique using the metaphor of the surgical knife: "Although Malcolm identified whites as the ones most responsible for the suffering of blacks, he did not absolve the victims from responsibility. He often appeared more angry with blacks for accepting exploitation than he was with whites who he claimed were responsible for it. His reference to the truth as 'sharp,' 'like a two-edged sword,' was applied primarily to blacks. 'It cuts into you,' he told them. 'It causes you great pain, but if you can take the truth, it will cure you and save you from what otherwise would be certain death.' "[24] As physicians of the soul, we look not to diagnose pathology in the body but sociopathology and ideological pathology. And our normative source for social health is found in our sacred story as African Americans and as Adventists. But what is that story? Who has told it to us? Have they told all of the story or only a part of it?

When Princeton religion professor Eddie Glaude Jr. posted an announcement on the HuffPost website that read, "The Black Church Is Dead,"he started chatter that went beyond the blogosphere.[25] Ironically, Timothy Beal noted a similar issue on the same website about the King James Bible: "The King James Bible's 400th may well be its biggest birthday ever, but also its most poignant. For its end draws nigh. Sure, it'll hang around for a while, mostly in hotels and old folks homes. But it's not long for this world, at least in any form we'd recognize from the bookish years of its youth."[26] Beal focuses on the crisis that our digital age brings to cultural products that were designed for the age of print, but maybe there is an unexpected connection between the King James Version of the Bible and the African American, or black, church. I am suggesting that the possible end of the one may foretell the inevitable fate of the other. If Glaude and Beal are both right, the twist of fate (the King James Version of the Bible and the black church have a shared origin around the early seventeenth century) may be a fortuitous prediction of their similar destiny of doom in the twenty-first century.

However, to answer the question about whether the King James Bible will survive is a little easier than answering the question, Is the black church dead? Obviously, the term *dead* is used metaphorically and so is not to be taken literally. Still, we probably don't mean "dead" in the sense that church-growth scholars figuratively talk about church closures in the life cycle of congregations—churches developing from conception, birth, prime, and maturity to eventual death.[27] To talk about the "death" of the black church means much more than the closing down of a local storefront worship center. The metaphorical death of this amorphous entity called the black church is much more akin to losing the "soul" of a cultural movement that has been co-opted by different values driven by social and economic change.[28]

Supporting black theology:
A conceptual framework for applying caring techniques

What has this to do with the surgical knife of African American Adventist healing shepherds? We must not forget that the Christian religion has two parents—Hellenism and Judaism.[29] In the same way, black theologians have recently come to realize that black Christianity also has two parents—African traditional religions and biblical apostolic faith.[30] When African American Christians of any denomination lose their story in the homogenous story of white Christians, they also lose the critical voice of their prophetic call. Theology is about story. Theology is about history. Black theology, even black Adventist theology, is about our story and our history uncensored. James Cone, the father of black liberation theology, notes, "Our denominational histories could hardly stand the test of critical scholarship, for they were written from the perspective of a particular ecclesiastical history and for the purpose of glorifying its leaders."[31] Why is there not more work among young African American Adventists that tells the story of the Advent movement through the workings of Richard Allen and other captive and free black people who awaited the coming of Christ?

James Cone's critique is reminiscent of Carter G. Woodson's charge that "Negros are taught to admire the Hebrew, the Greek, the Latin and the Teuton and to despise the African."[32] This also resonates with Frantz Fanon, who wrote of the French Caribbean, "The Black schoolboy in the Antilles, who in his lessons is forever talking about 'our ancestors, the Gauls,' identifies himself with the explorer."[33] This critique is the surgical knife. Do young African American Adventist healing shepherds have the courage to make the incision? Can a new generation of black Adventist theologians engage in a transparent, self-critical reflection? Are we able to reimagine our theological roots? Here is a fact: first and foremost, we come from a people whose faith was nurtured in the womb of the "invisible institution" better known as slave religion. Have black Adventists embraced black religion as a valued source for doing our theological reflection? This means more than embracing African American liturgical exuberance. If we intend to understand a black Adventist theological identity as offering a distinct contribution to the theological construction of the Adventist people, it takes more than reciting the joys of our expressive musical worship tradition.

> Theology is about story.
> Theology is about history.
> Black theology, even black Adventist theology, is about our story and our history uncensored.

To reimagine our theological heritage requires our ideological liberation. The metaphor of liberation can be sociopolitical or cultural.[34] I might add that liberation can also be theological. The courage to fully embrace a black American theological heritage signals the difference between "what it [means] to be a black Christian as opposed to what it [means] to be a white Christian in blackface."[35] We are grateful that white Adventist Christians tell the story of the Advent movement,[36] but we also have a story to tell. African American Adventists would abort the important development of a black cultural identity by allowing themselves to be seduced into some mythical universal Adventist theological heritage. Again, Frantz Fanon offers an apt warning: "There is a drama there, and the black intellectuals are running the risk of being trapped by it. What? I have barely opened eyes that had been blindfolded, and someone already wants to drown me in the universal? What about the others? Those who 'have no voice,' those who have no 'spokesman.' . . . I need to lose myself in my negritude, to see the fires, the segregations, the repressions, the rapes, the discriminations, the boycotts. We need to put our fingers on every sore that mottles the black uniform."[37]

A people cannot shepherd a multicultural discourse if they are not free to affirm their own culture. As we tell our story, let's remain respectful of the ways other Adventist people groups tell the story of a somehow shared Adventist identity. Our respect must remain even when their way of telling the story sounds so different from the ways we imagine it to be. And yes, respect also means challenging the telling of the story but doing so in the unmistakable spirit of Christ's love.

So then, we are healing shepherds. We are pastors. If we do not model how to shepherd this discourse with grace in our own Adventist community, we rightly have no part in being the deep-change, transformative healers in a world looking for leadership out of our toxic-discourse practices.

So what should we revisit in the story? How do we employ the black religious tradition to help tell the story of Adventism? We have had a good deal of discussion about our political battles for ecclesiastical parity. Dr. Lorenzo H. Grant has well documented the patterns of institutional racism. He also notes the decision of black

Adventists to opt for organizational accommodationism.[38] The question for the new generation of black Adventist theologians is, How much theological accommodationism remains because of our failure to challenge the story of our theological roots? Nearly a decade after Grant wrote his thesis, Dr. Calvin Rock wrote,

> Since the theological contours of Adventism have been provided by white and not black theologians, it is not surprising that Adventism's political perspective has little relevance for the minorities within its membership. . . . Black Seventh-day Adventists have basically two options; they can accept a foreign word (God's word to white theologians) as His word to them, or they can find (hear) the Word as it relates to them specifically. Such a Word is what black theology is all about. Black Seventh-day Adventists must come to understand that there is no such thing as "plain theology" or a theology which comes to one unconditioned by the hearer's social and political perspective.[39]

Included in these attempts to rethink and recast our theological roots in Adventism is Dr. Delbert Baker.[40] His study of William Ellis Foy joins the bolder tradition of those voices who have attempted to revisit our theological roots. This also includes men such as Dr. David Taylor and Dr. Ricardo Graham. We need more such voices today.

Reimaging the Bible as a source for nurturing social solidarity
In his book on pastoral theology, James H. Harris writes regarding the black church and its Christian educational agenda, "The first order of business for the church is to deprogram the clergy and laity who are victims of miseducation and self-hatred manifested in their tendency to regard too highly the ideas and practices of whites. Too many fail to appreciate their own culture, history, and tradition. A number of blacks are still reading the Bible and teaching through the

eyes of whites, failing to capture and transmit to others the sense of liberation and hope that runs throughout the Bible."[41]

What assumptions must we respectfully challenge as we rethink the theological roots of the Christian story in America? In 1619, when the "first permanent English settlement in America"[42] tested the fortitude of a stolen people, we discover that it also revealed the subversive power of the "Authorized" text of Holy Scripture. For most of the Africans, the Christian sacred story initially came as an oral tradition. This story was informed by the language of the King James Version. The telling of this story played a role in forming a people who were no people. How the African people appropriated that story reveals both the subversive and the discursive power of the Africans' use of the King James Version.

The scholars who translated the Bible into the King's English could not have imagined that their work would have such a profound impact on the formation of a community of abducted adults and kidnapped youth. They couldn't possibly have expected that the text of Scripture would serve to provide a language-world for those captives who came from vastly different areas of an enormous continent and struggled to find a common language and culture that would enable them to transcend a coerced identity as chattel.[43] European Americans would learn from their brothers and sisters in captivity just how subversive to human political, economic, and religious institutions the Christian story really is.

These African peoples, through a process of miscegenation and enculturation, became African Americans. This becoming is in part due to how they appropriated the Bible as an instrument in their fight for liberation. It was the modern forces of material greed that corrupted, even further, an already depraved economic system. Religious clerics sedated the disturbed Christian psyche by assuring the European religious mind and spirit that the Bible condoned the practice of African enslavement.[44] The combination

of a perverted theological tradition along with the economic bene-
fits of the trans-African slave trade influenced the founding fathers
of the United States of America
to author a pro-slavery document
as the legal basis upon which the
nation was constituted.[45] The Free
African Society, founded by black
men in Philadelphia, Pennsylvania
(before the United States Consti-
tutional Convention), anticipated
that the document coming out of
that momentous convention would
protect the civil rights of those

> For African Americans, their
> community was formed in,
> and by, the language-world
> of the Bible. Their faith was
> forged in, and through, the
> fires of slave religion.

patriots of European descendants but not those of its Negro patriots. From the start, African Americans fought for civil rights with
scarce material resources. The Bible became the material basis of a
spiritual resource for the forming and burgeoning community. And
how they used it tells us as much about the true spirit of the sacred
Scriptures as it does about the religion of the enslaved.

The formation of the African American people, a people whose
cultural heritage emerged around the language-world of a sacred text,
can teach the Christian world today a new way of viewing diverse
communities and what it means to be the church. What is the relationship between the Bible and the church? The historical debate
between Roman Catholics and Protestants has centered on the old
question—Which came first, the Bible or the church?[46] Catholics
argue that the church created the Bible. Protestants argue that the
Bible created the church. Catholics invoke the authority of church
tradition, an authority to decide what is acceptable as Bible. Protestants invoke the principle of *sola Scriptura*, the Bible alone, as the
rule for faith and practice, authorizing it to decide how to define the
church.

African Americans expose this as a false either/or dilemma. From African American history, we can see that the Bible did not form a church, nor did African Americans (as a cultural community or a community of faith) produce the Bible. For African Americans, their community was formed in, and by, the language-world of the Bible. Their faith was forged in, and through, the fires of slave religion. And as they heard the stories of Jesus, they identified His suffering with their suffering, His death with their death, His resurrection with their resurrection. Thus, their spirits were renewed, and their faith in God revived.

This came as good news. For a people of struggle (in their new-world existence), they are not doing the work, but they make the Bible work for them. It helped solidify their peoplehood. This power of Christian faith offers a third way for understanding what it means to be the church. For African Americans, no, the church did not create the Bible! For African Americans, the Bible was a given even before slave religion had morphed into an indigenous American Christianity. For African Americans, no, the Bible did not create the church! African Americans did not believe in Jesus because of the Bible; they believed in the Bible because of a living encounter with the risen Christ. For these sojourning children under heaven, the Bible first creates the community, and the community then creates the church. And the church ultimately uses the Bible as a toolbox. And it should continue to do so as long as it serves the pastoral purposes of healing, sustaining, and guiding.[47]

For African Americans, the Bible was more like the scaffolding from which they could frame any and all their beliefs. Not only did the King James Version provide a new, New World, a "language-world,"[48] but it also provided the psychic space for those enslaved people who needed to find their creative energy. And create these people did! The Bible became that inexhaustible cistern to which they would constantly return.

The Bible was first that source from which their folk rhymes and cultural traditions emerged. An example is found in the Negro parody on the Lord's Prayer:

"Our Fadder, Which are in Heaben!"—
White man owe me leben and pay me seben.
"D'y Kingdom come! D'y Will be done!"—
An' if I hadn't tuck dat, I wouldn' git none.[49]

They could draw on the Bible as a resource to craft sermons of hope and songs of resistance, as witnessed in James Weldon Johnson's seven sermons in verse entitled *God's Trombones*:

O Lord, we come this morning
Knee-bowed and body-bent
Before thy throne of grace.
O Lord—this morning—
Bow our hearts beneath our knees,
And our knees in some lonesome valley.

Mount your milk-white horse,
And ride-a this morning. . . .

And now, O Lord, this man of God,
Who breaks the bread of life this morning—
Shadow him in the hollow of thy hand . . .
Wash him with hyssop inside and out . . .
And set his tongue on fire.[50]

The Bible became a source for inspiring hymnody—the sacred music of the Negro spirituals:

There is a balm in Gilead,
To make the spirit whole.
There is a balm in Gilead,
To heal the sin-sick soul.[51]

The African American Church could now employ the Bible for crafting new sacred and secular texts. Like a scaffold, the King James Version Bible was a tool for forming a community of disinherited forced-labor migrant workers. Once the community was formed, the text served to create other texts: some secular, others sacred, some for sermons, others for song, some for healing, and others for resistance; nevertheless, all public texts for the benefit of the people.

African American Adventist shepherds:
A healing heritage of social justice

What assumptions must we respectfully challenge as we rethink the theological roots of the Adventist Christian story? Should we challenge the Eurocentric basis of Uriah Smith's eschatological misreading of the land in John's Apocalypse? Smith advances an argument about the second beast of Revelation 13 that completely ignores the genocide that took place in this land with respect to the native populations. He says of the land beast: "It symbolizes the United States. Another consideration pointing to the locality of this power is drawn from the fact that John saw it rising from the earth. If the sea, from which the leopard beast arose (Rev. 13:1), denotes peoples, nations, and multitudes (Rev. 17:15), the earth would suggest, by contrast, a new and previously unoccupied territory."[52] I am sure that the scores of millions of natives in the Western Hemisphere who died through war, disease, and enslavement were unaware that this territory, new to the European explorers, was unoccupied. Should we challenge, respectfully and in Christian love, the Eurocentric basis of early Adventist eschatology?

Should we also challenge current Adventist historians' misdirected focus on the social milieu of restorationism/primitivism as the theological context of Adventist identity?[53] There is a real failure of religious historians in America to recognize Richard Allen as the person who carries the true spirit of the reformers.[54] The fog of distortion lifted for Cone when he wrote, "I began to think that what Richard Allen, the founder of the AME Church, did during the late eighteenth and early nineteenth centuries was as revolutionary as what Martin Luther did in the sixteenth century."[55] Maybe the focus of the social justice contributions offered from the "silent institution" of slave religion provides a better starting place for black Adventist theologians to work from!

Again, should we respectfully challenge the notion that William Miller and his movement reclaimed the lost doctrine of Christ's return? We know from the hymns of Isaac Watts and the writings of Bishop Ussher that the premillennial expectation of Jesus' return predates William Miller by centuries. What is less known is that the hope of a premillennial return of Christ was sustained in the hearts of the enslaved community of Christ's oppressed disciples. Richard Allen's pre-1801 hymn entitled "Spiritual Song" is a positive indication that black Christianity continued to treasure the doctrine of the return of Jesus. Furthermore, it was this doctrine that served as a catalyst for their exuberant and expressive worship. Members from the African American religious community contributed to the ethos of the Second Great Awakening even before there was a Millerite movement.[56] Bishop Richard Allen's words to his hymn "Spiritual Song" indicate a theology of the return of Jesus. He composes the first stanza:

Good morning brother Pilgrim, what marching to Zion . . .
Feel you a desire that burns like a fire,
And longs for the hour that Christ shall appear.

The tenth stanza continues this eschatological theme:

Our time is a-flying, our moments a-dying,
We are led to improve them and quickly appear,
For the bless'd hour when Jesus in power,
In glory shall come is now drawing near.

Maybe the theology in the spirituals served as the real impetus for the reemergence of the doctrine of the return of Christ. Maybe this hope remained in black Christians because of these captives' unquenchable thirst for divine justice.[57] It is very possible that the dark complexion of a minority African people in this majority European colony signaled that there was no hiding place over here. Nevertheless, they sang about an all-seeing God, who watches the deeds of humanity, and they knew they were not the only ones subject to the gaze of another. So they sang:

Dere's no hidin' place down dere,
Dere's no hidin' place down dere,
Oh I went to de rock to hide my face,
De rock cried out, "No hidin' place," . . .
Oh de rock cried, "I'm burnin' too," . . .
I want to go to hebbin as well as you,"
Dere's no hidin' place down dere.[58]

The question for us today is: Will our theological re-storying remain a tool for healing in the hands of this unique and modern people? Story has shaped a modern peoples' identity; nevertheless, identities are malleable. We construct them, and then we reconstruct them. We do this in the same way that we revise our sacred narratives. We write them, and we rewrite them. The religious consciousness of Africans and African Americans realized that the text that was always bound in leather and locked in sacred buildings was a text still open to a new future. The stories in them continue to speak to the reality of new possibilities. Our realizing of those possibilities allows the text to live on. This text of reformation, we now know, has done the unexpected work of formation—forming the people now known as African Americans. Maybe we can appropriate it to another task—the task of transformative healing, transforming the faithful ecclesial communities who read it, hear it, and do its bidding.

Maury Jackson

Maury Jackson is the associate dean of the HMS Richards Divinity School at La Sierra University, associate professor of Practical Theology, chair of the Pastoral Studies Department, and coordinator of the philosophical studies program. He is an ordained Seventh-day Adventist minister. Formerly, he served as adjunct assistant professor of philosophy for the Antelope Valley College, in Lancaster, California, and served the Southern California Conference of Seventh-day Adventists as pastor in the Lancaster Adventist Church and the Ojai Valley Adventist Church. He teaches courses in homiletics, applied pastoral theology, and ethics. A graduate of La Sierra University, Andrews University, California State University Los Angeles, and Claremont School of Theology; he received the degrees of Bachelor of Arts in Religion, Master of Divinity, Master of Arts in Philosophy, and Doctor of Ministry.

1. Desmond Ford, *Physicians of the Soul: God's Prophets Through the Ages* (Nashville, TN: Southern Publishing Association, 1980).

2. Harriet A. Washington, *Medical Apartheid: The Dark History of Medical Experimentation on Black Americans From Colonial Times to the Present* (New York: Anchor Books, 2008), 47.

3. James H. Harris, *Pastoral Theology: A Black-Church Perspective* (Minneapolis: Fortress, 1991), 55, 56.

4. While practical theologians have approached their research under these assumptions for some time, black theologians while consciously employing this method are not as explicit about their theological project being linked to practical theological studies. While not a theist, Anthony Pinn is a great example of the task that black theologians (who take their context seriously as a locus for divine revelation) should be about. See Anthony

B. Pinn, *The End of God-Talk: An African American Humanist Theology* (Oxford: Oxford University Press, 2012), 9–43.

5. Jon Michael Spencer, *Theological Music: Introduction to Theomusicology* (New York: Greenwood, 1991), 8.

6. Richard Delgado, ed., *Critical Race Theory: The Cutting Edge* (Philadelphia: Temple University Press, 1995).

7. Ian F. Haney Lopez, "The Social Construction of Race," in Delgado, 194.

8. Craig R. Prentiss, ed., *Religion and the Creation of Race and Ethnicity: An Introduction* (New York: New York University Press, 2003), 3.

9. "With an emphasis upon the way stories are used in society, we are defining as myth a narrative that not only claims truth for itself but is also seen by a community as credible and authoritative. . . . So, according to this definition, stories achieve the status of myth among a given people by the way they are *used*. These stories bind groups of people, providing common reference points from which they may negotiate various facets of their lives." Prentiss, 5.

10. Wayne Proudfoot, *Religious Experience* (Berkeley: University of California Press, 1985), 42.

11. Paul Harvey, "A Servant of Servants Shall He Be," in Prentiss, *Religion and the Creation of Race*, 14.

12. This was the title of Carter G. Woodson's famous book.

13. Lerone Bennett Jr., *Before the Mayflower: A History of Black America* (New York: Penguin Books, 1988), 29.

14. Ivan Van Sertima, *They Came Before Columbus: The African Presence in Ancient America* (New York: Random House, 2003).

15. Cheikh Anta Diop, *The African Origin of Civilization: Myth or Reality*, ed. and trans. Mercer Cook, (Chicago, IL: Lawrence Hill Books, 1974). See also Albert J. Raboteau, *Slave Religion: The "Invisible Institution" in the Antebellum South* (New York: Oxford University Press, 1978).

16. While the actual complexion of the peoples of ancient North Africa cannot be conclusively determined, Frank Snowden suggests that we may be able to infer from a third century BCE Etruscan coin (that shows the head of a Negro on the obverse and an elephant on the reverse) that ancient North Africans would be considered black under the modern racial scheme. See Frank M. Snowden Jr., *Before Color Prejudice: The Ancient View of Blacks* (Cambridge, MA: Harvard University Press, 1983), illustration 31a, b.

17. Although it is considered that Moses was a monotheist, a good case has been made (by Harry Emerson Fosdick) that the early Hebrew people are more accurately to be described as henotheist: they believed in the existence of other gods but were to worship only Yahweh. Compare Harry Emerson Fosdick, *A Guide to Understanding the Bible: The Development of Ideas Within the Old and New Testaments* (New York: Harper & Row, 1967).

18. Henry H. Mitchell, *Black Church Beginnings: The Long-Hidden Realities of the First Years* (Grand Rapids, MI: William B. Eerdmans, 2004), 17.

19. Lerone Bennett Jr., *Before the Mayflower: A History of Black America* (New York: Penguin Books, 1988), 29.

20. Vincent L. Wimbush, *The Bible and African Americans: A Brief History* (Minneapolis: Fortress, 2003), 12–20.

21. Wimbush, 17.

22. Henri J. M. Nouwen, *The Wounded Healer: Ministry in Contemporary Society* (New

York: Image Books Doubleday, 1979).

23. Robert J. C. Young, *Postcolonialism: A Very Short Introduction* (New York: Oxford University Press, 2003), 128, 129.

24. James Cone, *Martin & Malcolm & America: A Dream or a Nightmare* (Maryknoll, NY: Orbis Books, 1992), 98.

25. Eddie Glaude Jr., "The Black Church Is Dead," HuffPost, updated August 23, 2012, http://www.huffingtonpost.com/eddie-glaude-jr-phd/the-black-church-is-dead_b_473815.html.

26. Timothy Beal, "Will the King James Bible Survive?" HuffPost, updated May 25, 2011, http://www.huffingtonpost.com/timothy-beal/happy-400th-birthday-king_b_836538.html.

27. Martin F. Saarinen, *The Life Cycle of a Congregation* (Bethesda, MD: The Alban Institute, 2001), 6, 7, 22.

28. Michael Jinkins, *The Church Faces Death: Ecclesiology in a Post-Modern Context* (New York: Oxford University Press, 1999).

29. Walter Rauschenbusch, *Christianity and the Social Crisis* (Louisville, KY: Westminster John Knox, 1907), 107.

30. James H. Cone, *For My People: Black Theology and the Black Church* (Maryknoll, NY: Orbis Books, 1984), 62. See also Henry H. Mitchell, *Black Church Beginnings: The Long-Hidden Realities of the First Years* (Grand Rapids, MI: William B. Eerdmans, 2004), chapters 1, 2.

31. Cone, 60.

32. Carter G. Woodson, *The Mis-Education of the Negro* (Chicago, IL: African American Images, 2000), 1.

33. Frantz Fanon, *Black Skin White Masks*, trans. Charles Lam Markmann (New York: Grove Press, 1967), 147.

34. Cone, *For My People*, 62. See also James H. Cone, *My Soul Looks Back* (Maryknoll, NY: Orbis Books, 1986), 112.

35. Jeremiah A. Wright Jr., "Protestant Ecclesiology," in *The Cambridge Companion to Black Theology*, ed. Dwight N. Hopkins and Edward P. Antonio (Cambridge, UK: Cambridge University Press, 2012), 188. "It is not surprising to see that he [the white man] identifies himself with the Negro: white 'hot-jazz' orchestras, white blues and spiritual singers, white authors writing novels in which the Negro proclaims his grievances, whites in blackface." Fanon, *Black Skin White Masks*, 177.

36. Martin Weber, *Who's Got the Truth: Making Sense Out of Five Different Adventist Gospels* (Columbia, MD: Calvary Connections, 1995). Lest one be mistaken by the myth that there is only one Adventist theology, Weber details the theological varieties of five different Adventist theologians—represented are Morris Venden, George Knight, Jack Sequeira, Ralph Larson, and Graham Maxwell.

37. Frantz Fanon, *Black Skin White Masks*, trans. Charles Lam Markmann, (New York: Grove Press, 1967), 186, 187.

38. Lorenzo H. Grant, "The Origin and Development of Black Conferences in the Seventh-day Adventist Church" (master's thesis, Howard University, 1976).

39. Calvin B. Rock, "Institutional Loyalty Versus Racial Freedom: The Dilemma of Black Seventh-day Adventist Leadership" (PhD diss., Vanderbilt University, 1984).

40. Delbert W. Baker, *The Unknown Prophet: Before Ellen White God Used William Ellis Foy* (Hagerstown, MD: Review and Herald®, 1987).

41. Harris, *Pastoral Theology*, 112.

42. Bennett, *Before the Mayflower*, 29.

43. Wimbush, *Bible and African Americans*, 1–11.

44. W. E. B. Du Bois, *The Negro Church* (Walnut Creek, CA: ALTAMIRA, 2003), 6–12.

45. Ronald Osborn, *Anarchy and Apocalypse: Essays on Faith, Violence, and Theodicy* (Eugene, OR: Cascade Books, 2010), 74.

46. Elizabeth A. Livingstone, ed., *The Concise Oxford Dictionary of the Christian Church* (Oxford: Oxford University Press, 1977), 519.

47. Seward Hiltner, *Preface to Pastoral Theology: The Ministry and Theory of Shepherding* (Nashville: Abingdon, 1954), 15–29.

48. Wimbush, *Bible and African Americans*, 1.

49. Dudley Randall, ed., *The Black Poets: A New Anthology* (Toronto: Bantam Books, 1971), 5.

50. James Weldon Johnson, *God's Trombones: Seven Negro Sermons in Verse* (New York: Penguin Classics, 1976), 11, 12.

51. Johnson, 86.

52. Uriah Smith, *Daniel and the Revelation: The Response of History to the Voice of Prophecy—A Verse by Verse Study of these Important Books of the Bible* (Nashville, TN: Southern Publishing Association, 1897), 573.

53. George R. Knight, *A Search for Identity: The Development of Seventh-day Adventist Beliefs* (Hagerstown, MD: Review and Herald®, 2000), 30–37.

54. Cone, *My Soul Looks Back*, 27.

55. Cone, 27.

56. Kenneth L. Waters Sr., "Liturgy, Spirituality, and Polemic in the Hymnody of Richard Allen," *The North Star: A Journal of African American Religious History* 2, no. 2 (Spring 1999).

57. James H. Cone, *The Spirituals and the Blues: An Interpretation* (Maryknoll, NY: Orbis Books, 2004), 92–96.

58. Cone, *Spirituals and the Blues*, 94.

CALVIN B. ROCK

Healed by Something Better

The principle of "something better" is nestled in Hebrews 11:39, 40 and is mentioned no less than eleven times in this book's memorable portrayal of the means whereby Christ reconciles lost humanity.[1] "And these all, having obtained a good report through faith, received not the promise: God having provided some better thing for us, that they without us should not be made perfect" (KJV). Likewise, history reveals that the principle of "something better," nestled in the human heart, is a true and traceable cause of humanity's most noble and productive energies.

We see this concept of "something better" at work in the founding of our nation, whose pilgrims were drawn to these shores in search of religious and political freedom. We see it in the history of our church, whose pioneers assembled from various "post-Reformation groups" in response to newfound truth. And we see the hope of "something better" at work in the remarkable climb of the descendants of American slavery to their present status. As we consider the role of black Americans as healers in today's multicultural society, we also celebrate appropriately the healing they themselves have experienced by the elevating, innervating power of "something better."

Previously without hope

While many of the ships that brought slaves to these shores had such suggestive names as *The Liberty*, *The Desire*, *The Brotherhood*, and the *Good Ship Jesus*, their human cargo had no such outlook. Shoved in and shackled together for weeks in the putrid bellies of rolling ships, those who survived were disgorged upon these shores besieged and bewildered, weakened and wanting. They were shoved upon auction blocks where they were poked, prodded, beaten, bartered, and delivered into the most hopeless brand of slavery known to human history.

What distinguished American slavery, making it so depressingly unique, is that it had no "manumission," no exit clause. From as far back as Hebrew slavery, as noted in the book of Exodus, the cruelest of slave systems had provisions whereby, ostensibly at least, slaves could gain their freedom by an accumulation of earnings or years of service. There was no such allowance in the slave codes of America. As a result, slaves were forced to labor day after depressing day, year after weary year, decade after dreary decade, with no hope or possibility of something better.

Often fed like animals at troughs where they thrust their grimy fingers into the mush hoping to gain strength for yet another day of unrequited labor, they worked in tattered rags, slept on muddy floors, and rose each morning to function at the mercy of avaricious, often rapacious masters. Destined to live and die in this pit of misery without a sliver of hope, these slaves had brief lives that contained no rainbow of deliverance, no ray of freedom, no light at the end of the tunnel. They were a race for whom, as one poet put it, "hope unborn had died." For them, there was no hint of healing or hint of "something better."

A glimmer of hope

None, that is, until in 1671, when the Bible's promise of a better life in a world to come was brought to a small number of slaves on a Virginia plantation by a group of Friends, or Quakers. They were followed in 1701 by The Society for the Propagation of the Gospel in Foreign Parts, a Christian forum based in England; the Episcopal Church in 1705; the Anglican Church in 1727; the Methodist Church in 1780; and the Presbyterian Church in 1794. These brave missionaries risked their lives when infiltrating the properties of slave owners with the news of "something better," as did the slaves who dared connect and listen.

> The good news, rudimentary as it was, stirred in their hearts visions of freedom that gave birth to singing and a brand-new genre of music later labeled the Negro spiritual.

Nevertheless, slaves found clever means to communicate with their benefactors and spread the good news across the cotton rows in whispered excitement and from plantation to plantation by the coded beat of their speaking drums. The good news, rudimentary as it was, stirred in their hearts visions of freedom that gave birth to singing and a brand-new genre of music later labeled the Negro spiritual.

Knowing that their masters would not be pleased, they turned their cooking pots upside down to mute their voices and sang with soulful joy, "Up above my head I hear music in the air," "Swing low, sweet chariot, coming for to carry me home," and "Steal away, steal away, steal away to Jesus. . . . I ain't got long to stay here."

Our prophet, Ellen White, affirmed the reality of many slave conversions when in portraying the scenes of the Second Coming, she wrote: "Then commenced the jubilee, when the land should rest. I saw the pious slave rise in victory and triumph, and shake off the chains that bound him, while his wicked master was in confusion and knew not what to do."[2]

Not surprisingly, the ennobling power of "something better" soon generated in their hearts a determination for deliverance in this life as well. The few masters who thought that teaching them Bible verses would suppress any desire for "something better" were on the wrong side of scriptural dynamism. Those masters who sought to keep them from Scripture lest it stir them to rebellion had it right because, inevitably, in the sequence of godly urgings, the "Thy kingdom come" appeal for future bliss is a precursor to the "give us this day our daily bread" plea for present satisfaction. It was thus preordained and predictable that the biblical principle of "something better" would drive the slaves to overt resistance. And it did so in a number of ways.

A response born of desperation

The first was a spate of physical attacks spearheaded by zealous slave leaders who led their ragtag followers in violent revolution against their owners. Principal among them was Gabriel Prosser (Virginia, 1800), who, inspired by Judges 15, saw himself as the Black Samson, commissioned to lead God's ill-equipped people against highly superior foes. Another was Denmark Vesey (South Carolina, 1822), who, charged by the life of Moses' successor, proclaimed himself as the Black Joshua. Most notable of all was Nat Turner (Virginia, 1830), who, when trapped and caught after considerable bloodshed, was asked moments before he was hanged if he had any final words. He replied with convicted resolution, "They hanged Jesus, didn't they?"

A second, more practical way in which the "something better" principle generated resistance was the Underground Railroad that spirited thousands of slaves from the cotton fields of the South all the way north to the snowy fields of Canada. The conductors who led slaves through and around dangers were Christians; the stations where they were temporarily housed were Christian churches, homes, and barns. Hiding by day and following their starry GPS by night, they waded through mosquito-infested swamps, evading bounty hunters and baying bloodhounds, bravely trudging tirelessly on to freedom.

The third and most determinative assault upon the institution of slavery fueled by the "something better" dynamic was manifested in the aggressive approaches of the abolitionist movement (1835–1865). Abolitionists came in two categories: Christian terrorists and Christian pacificists. Christian terrorists included individuals such as John Brown, the fiery Puritan preacher and architect of the ill-fated Harper's Ferry, Virginia, raid in 1859. Along with his colleagues, he was captured and hanged, riding to the gallows on the coffin so soon to receive his remains.

Chief of the Christian pacifists was journalist William Lloyd Garrison. Abolitionists in this category were pastors, educators, editors, and statesmen who wrote and spoke with great passion against human bondage and who, with the superior weaponry of moral sanctioning, successfully pricked the country's conscience, hastening slavery's demise.

The influence of the Christian church with its scripturally inspired mandate of "something better" did not cease with the end of slavery. It operated with needed efficiency after the nineteenth century as well.

After emancipation

With the coming of emancipation, four million freed slaves (twice the number of captives that fled Pharaoh's Egypt), 95 percent of all blacks then in the United States, were set adrift in the land, the vast majority unlettered and unskilled. They were, for the most part, a mass of hapless, homeless, helpless wanderers.

The bitter resentment of their former masters coupled with their vulnerability made their plight in some ways worse than their former lot—except for the psychological damage of slavery. They had been ushered into freedom under the protecting watch of the Union army. But they had no Moses to lead them, no pillar of cloud by day or pillar of fire by night.

Compounding their plight was the removal of the Federal troops from the South in 1876 by President Rutherford B. Hayes in fulfillment of his promise to do so if the South would vote for him. In 1896, twenty years later, the establishment of the "separate but equal" doctrine in the case of *Plessey v. Ferguson* further compounded the misery of former slaves and their descendants.

Early on, the white church, primarily in the North, led out in the healing process; there was no black church. However, in 1787 the first black Christian congregation, naming itself the African Methodist Episcopal Church, was organized in Philadelphia. Other black congregations followed during the next three decades. By 1918, at the end of World War I, what became known as the black Christian church, with its many branches, was fully operative.

That group, which today claims approximately 80 percent of all black American Christians (generously aided by their white Christian counterparts), provided the primary principles and personnel for African American protest and progress during the twentieth century.

That support was direly needed not only in the South but also in the North, which is where southern blacks migrated in huge numbers at the time of World War I. Pushed on the one hand by nature's droughts and human cruelty and pulled on the other by the promise of factory jobs and social freedom, they made their way from "down South" to "down North," as Martin Luther King Jr. would later derisively label it, only to find themselves unprepared for the bitter cold of winter, the crowded landscape, and the ever-present reality of urban crime.

Then came the 1930s and the awful depression years, followed by the 1940s, during which World War II produced more factory jobs and a second great migration of blacks, with a repetition and compounding of the woes encountered in the first. After that came the 1950s and 1960s with the bitter, bloody riots before, during, and after the triumphs of the civil rights movement.

In the latter years of the century just ended and during the early years of the twenty-first century, African Americans have continued to face challenges of poverty, joblessness, lack of skills education, lack of prenatal and elderly care, and the crippling lack of access to health care in general.

While it is accurate to say that the Christian church has through the decades been foremost among the institutions of the land in the healing of black America, that is not to say that the church has done all that it could have or should have done. But in comparison with all other institutions, its grades are clearly superior.

A positive legacy

It was the Christian community that first said no to the sin of slavery and yes to its disenfranchised survivors. During the decades following slavery, when blacks were denied attendance at the colleges and universities of the land, it was the church that founded a broad system of "faith-based" educational institutions (primarily in the South). H. Richard Niebuhr, in his book *The Social Sources of Denominationalism*, describes their birth as "mushrooms springing up after a summer rain."[3]

It was the church in 1905 that supplied the charter members of the Niagara Movement, later to become the National Association for the Advancement of Colored People (NAACP). The church also supplied the civil rights movement of the 1950s and 1960s its primary spokespersons, its transportation system, its meeting houses, and its many marchers and martyrs, black and white.

And how did we, the Seventh-day Adventist Church, relate to the needs encountered by this people, the only minority in the land brought here against its will? The only racial group whose males were castrated for spite and lynched for sport? The cultural unit whose women were so abused by their masters as to, along with later mixing with various Indian tribes, effectively eliminate the pure African strain that was brought here, resulting in the redefinition of the slave descendants from "African" to "Colored"? The group decreed by the Supreme Court in the famous Dred Scott case of 1857 as having "no rights which the white man was bound to respect"?[4] The only group in American history whose individuals, as voted by the infamous Philadelphia compromise of July 1787, were legally declared to be three-fifths of a person? The group that has for most of American history been the last ones hired and the first ones fired? The group who, largely because of the many boundary-maintaining mechanisms (formal and informal) structured by the nation, have proven insoluble in the cultural melting pot proposed by Thomas Jefferson as America's social ideal?

The Adventist connection

Our church's contribution, given the time of its origin (1863), began as slavery was ending and is a matter of good news and bad news. The bad news is that, as is the case with most churches having a high degree of apocalyptic expectation, our theologians tended to limit the "something better" principle—first by framing it as a strictly spiritual notion and second (and just as crippling), by relegating it to the "kingdom come," what the cynics have coined as "pie in the sky by and by."

The result is that the Adventist Church has historically functioned within the parameters of the government's decisions regarding such issues as the fugitive slave law, separate but equal, racial quotas, miscegenation, voting rights, and the like. Change has usually come only after the government has admitted its errors and changed its laws.

That includes opening our institution's doors (hospitals, churches, and schools) to all only after the government's overthrow of "separate but equal" in Brown v. The Board of Education in 1954. Clearly, we preachers of prophecy, for the most part, have been far less than prophetic in regard to social justice.

The consequence in the African American sector of Adventism

has been much frustration and the loss of literally thousands whose understanding of God's "something better" in the "here and now" would not allow them permanence in a structure where this was not a priority.

But there is good news as well. The good news is that many of our founders, including John Byington, our first General Conference president, were abolitionists. *The Seventh-day Adventist Encyclopedia* states of Byington, elected to office in 1863, that in his early years, "he was actively antislavery in sentiment," also that "he regularly entertained Indians and Blacks in his home, and is said to have maintained a station of the Underground Railroad at Buck's Bridge, New York, where he lived on a farm."[5]

The good news is that our church prophet, Ellen White, from her earliest years of ministry, issued repeated rebukes against the slave trade and was so adamant a crusader for justice that she advocated civil disobedience rather than conformity to the evils of existing law. Her words were, "When the laws of men conflict with the word and law of God, we are to obey the latter, whatever the consequences may be. The law of our land requiring us to deliver a slave to his master, we are not to obey; and we must abide the consequences of violating this law."[6]

> Ellen White, from her earliest years of ministry, issued repeated rebukes against the slave trade and was so adamant a crusader for justice that she advocated civil disobedience rather than conformity to the evils of existing law.

The good news is that in spite of defections from the ranks of Adventism by several notable black leaders, we have not, as is the case with most recognized denominations, suffered a major organizational schism. This is largely because of the shining examples of such faithful church members as Ruth Janetta Temple, MD, who was born in Natchez, Mississippi, in 1892. She moved with her family to Los Angeles in 1904, and later, as a young adult, received a five-year scholarship to the College of Medical Evangelists, and in 1918 became the first black person to graduate from that institution, now known as Loma Linda University. Among other accomplishments, Temple began a clinic for the underserved in southeast Los Angeles, later named after her. She died in 1984, having remained a visible, loyal Seventh-day Adventist.

The good news is that we were blessed with a succession of highly visible ministerial leaders—white and black—whose preaching inspired unity of belief and fellowship. Evangelists Fordyce Detamore and H. M. S. Richards Sr. and Jr. are examples of Caucasian pastors who were forthright in this regard.

Within the black community itself, F. L. Peterson, the first black graduate of Pacific Union College (1916) and the first black general vice president of the world church (1962), and evangelists E. E. Cleveland and C. D. Brooks typify many whose preaching emphasis has been pivotal to the loyalty index of black Adventism.

The good news is that at critical periods of the past century, there were presidents of the General Conference who boldly urged the church forward in the matter of fairness. Two who stand out were W. H. Branson (1950–1954) and Neal C. Wilson (1968–1979). Branson's truly groundbreaking statement to the nation's union conference presidents and chairmen of sanitarium (hospital) and college boards on December 23, 1953, reads in part, "Seventh-day Adventists should not hold back any longer in this matter, but should step into the ranks of those organizations that are declaring themselves in favor of non-segregation in our schools and sanitariums."

The good news is that largely as a result of Branson's boldness and Wilson's wisdom, along with that of others, six of our nation's nine union conferences have (or have had) black presidents. These include the Atlantic, Columbia, Lake, Mid-America, Pacific, and Southern Union Conferences.

The good news is that the North American Division elected a black president, Charles E. Bradford, in 1979, three full decades before its territorial counterpart, the United States of America, would do so in the person of Barak Obama.

The good news is that the second female to serve as president of a Seventh-day Adventist college or university in the United States is an African American, Heather Knight, now at Pacific Union College.

The journey ahead

But is such evidence, including the appointment of our own Barry Black as chaplain of the United States Senate, or even the $170 million in tithe returned by African Americans in 2012, a sign that the patient, so badly wounded by 250 years of slavery and 90 years of legally imposed inferiority, has healed sufficiently so as to stop treatment? Or, to put it another way, that this group has achieved parity in terms of professional, political, and economic status in society and/or the church?

The answer is no—not while comprising 13 percent of the population and less than 4 percent in critical professions such as law and medicine. Not with 3 percent of PhD recipients and 40 percent of the jail population. Not while earning paychecks that are 30 percent less than the national average. Not with eight fewer years of longevity for men and seven fewer years for women compared with the national average and an infant mortality rate 2.3 times that of the national rate.

And in regard to the matter of interracial fellowship, have we achieved, or are we soon likely to achieve, a state of harmony that will allow us to relax or abandon our efforts for healing? Again, the answer is no. In fact, our prophet has warned: "The relation of the two races has been a matter hard to deal with, and I fear that it will ever remain a most perplexing problem."[7]

However, in spite of that knowledge and the hardwired social realities about us, we modern Christian abolitionists, if you please, are all of us under gospel obligation to work for "something better." And those efforts must involve better things than intermittent pronouncements regarding racial harmony. They should include, first of all, honest desegregation, an open-door policy for all, as opposed to forced integration or contrived assimilation. We should not feel guilty because ours is a flower garden rather than a monolithic society, especially given the fact that a so-called colorless society is sociologically impractical, organizationally untenable, and theologically unsubstantiated.

Critical to that view is our comfort with the knowledge that, as with the day of Pentecost, it is still a fact that each distinct culture hears the gospel best in its own socialized idiom. It is wrong to label a group "racist" or "segregationist" because its members choose to worship in that language without restrictions toward others.

Second, we can and must, while maintaining the standards of excellence for which our institutions are known, continue to expand our community-based services for the underprivileged. That should include not only "boots on the ground" ministries where people live but also on-campus programs that address practical needs—again without diluting operational excellence.

Third, our institutional calendars would do well to include year-round education programming involving all of its significant cultural components as a means of strengthening and healing relationships.

This is personal
On the very day of Barak Obama's first inauguration, my mother died at age ninety-six. Her mother, Etta Littlejohn, was a girl of fifteen when she heard the Adventist message from the decks of the *Morning Star*, the boat built by our prophet's son, Edson White, which he sailed down the Mississippi River for the purpose of educating the

children of recently freed slaves. Etta was one of the original sixteen students at what was then Oakwood Industrial School (the fortieth such school built by churches) when its doors opened in November 1896. She earned her nursing certificate and later served as one of Ellen White's chambermaids at the old Melrose sanitarium in the Boston area.

Etta married Robert L. Bradford, a Seventh-day Adventist minister, and became the mother of Eva, her fourth child (my mother); and Charles, her eighth and youngest (mentioned earlier). When my mother was an octogenarian, I invited her to speak at the Abundant Life Church in Las Vegas, where I was pastoring. When I asked her that morning about her topic, reminding her that it was a Black History Sabbath, her reply was, "Don't worry; I *am* black history." And she was. Born just forty-seven years after slavery and steeped in Adventism, she was an encyclopedia of historical information, an eyewitness to almost a century of transitional events in society and the church.

That reply also contained all the soulful pride of one whose great-grandfather's name was changed from Weems to Bradford—the name of a white family relocating from Alabama to Kansas. His parent placed him on their wagon, knowing that his opportunities for "something better" would be enhanced.

It was the answer of one whose years on earth doubled those that had intervened between the end of slavery and her birth, and who through those decades had witnessed her people's climb against staggering odds from the outhouse of legal discrimination to the White House of international recognition, a feat of faith and works enduringly fashioned by the call of "something better."

It is paradoxical, absolutely stunning, and unspeakably incomprehensible—in fact, humanly inconceivable—that Jesus was willing to undergo the exact reverse of that process in order to free us from the slavery of sin. He left the health and happiness of glory, the conduct of universal affairs, and the praise of adoring angels to save us from the slavery of sin and the tyranny of death. He came from opulence to obscurity, from riches to rags, from sovereignty to servanthood, to bear our griefs and carry our sorrows.

He came all-God and all-man. He was in all the right ways "separate but equal." His divinity was separate from ours but equal with the Father's. His sinless humanity was separate from ours but equal with unfallen Adam's. And at the end, He was separated by a cloud that engulfed Him in the final moments of His agony. But because He was equal with the law, He could, and did, took as our penalty for its breaking in His death. "He was wounded for our transgressions, he was bruised for our iniquities: the chastisement of our peace was upon him; and with his stripes we are healed" (Isaiah 53:5, KJV).

> It is paradoxical, absolutely stunning, and unspeakably incomprehensible—in fact, humanly inconceivable—that Jesus was willing to undergo the exact reverse of that process in order to free us from the slavery of sin.

By His precious blood, Jesus signed our emancipation proclamation and opened freedom's gates to all humanity. Then, mission accomplished, He ascended back to glory. But our Lord did not leave us comfortless; He did not pull out the troops. In fact, He sent reinforcements in the person of the Holy Spirit and promised never to leave us alone. Jesus pledged that even as He came down to represent the Father to us, He would represent us to the Father when He got home and, further, make a way that where He is, there we might be also.

Because of that, Jesus is not only the Courier of "something better," He *is* Something better! Hebrews affirms that Christ is a better Tabernacle; a better Hope; a better Resurrection; a better Reward; and, most meaningfully, a better Sacrifice, a better High Priest; Himself the Offering, Himself the Offered.

It is Christ's nailed-pierced hands, hands that now present to the Father His faultless blood as something better than our efforts for forgiveness, that offer us His righteous robe as something better than our relative perfection. It is into those nail-pierced hands that we lodge our pleas and rest our hopes—our pleas for tolerance to accept difference, for boldness to confront oppression, and our hope of His soon return and the inauguration of the peaceable kingdom where the redeemed will never cease their enhancement. As we now see through the glass darkly, we will then see our Savior face-to-face, ever reveling in untarnished fellowship with one another in unmarred, unmitigated, unbroken, unhindered, unwavering, unlimited, untroubled, untiring, unending communion with Him.

Calvin B. Rock

Dr. Rock was born in New York, New York, and is the product of Christian education including undergraduate studies at Oakwood College. His graduate studies were completed at the University of Detroit and Vanderbilt University where the degrees of DMin and PhD were conferred in Religious Ethics. He has served the Seventh-day Adventist Church for sixty years, his posts included pastor, evangelist, educator, administrator, and author.

---

1. Previously published as Calvin B. Rock, "Something Better," *Adventist Review*, February 5, 2021, https://www.adventistreview.org/something-better.

2. Ellen G. White, *Early Writings* (Washington, DC: Review and Herald®, 1945), 286.

3. H. Richard Niebuhr, *The Social Sources of Denominationalism* (New York: H. Holt, 1929).

4. "Dred Scott Case: The Supreme Court Decision," PBS, accessed August 9, 2021, https://www.pbs.org/wgbh/aia/part4/4h2933t.html.

5. Don Neufeld, ed., *The Seventh-day Adventist Encyclopedia*, vol. 10 of the Commentary Reference Series (Washington, DC: Review and Herald®, 1996), s.v. "Byington, John."

6. Ellen G. White, *Testimonies for the Church*, vol. 1 (Mountain View, CA: Pacific Press®, 1948), 201, 202.

7. Ellen G. White, *The Southern Work* (Washington, DC: Review and Herald®, 1966), 84.

LESLIE N. POLLARD, PhD, DMin, MBA

Conference Mission, Structure, and Function:

An Analysis of Organizational Unity and Mission Particularity in the North American Division of the Seventh-day Adventist Church

Recently, in the early 2000s, a number of writers and speakers have urged changes in the organizational structure of the North American Division[1] of Seventh-day Adventists (hereafter, NAD). These changes intend the dissolution of those entities within the NAD officially designated as "Regional conferences."[2] These calls have been forwarded in the stated interest of "unifying" the Adventist Church in North America. The continued existence of Regional conferences has evoked a variety of descriptors intended to stress the perception of "disunity" in the NAD due to the continued existence of these nine organizational units. Adventist writers or speakers have described the existence of Regional conference structures as "race-based organizational segregation,"[3] "Adventist apartheid,"[4] "the sin we don't want to overcome,"[5] "an abnormality,"[6] "a disgrace,"[7] "morally untenable,"[8] and "a lingering evil."[9]

Other writers and speakers have also urged the restructuring of the NAD, though in less evocative language. In the February 20, 1997, issue of the *Adventist Review*, David Williams suggested that the church should "eliminate *all* [emphasis added] of the current structures and build new ones based on new principles."[10] William Johnsson, in one of his final articles as editor of the *Adventist Review*, raised and answered the question, "What will it take to bring us together?"[11] Johnsson pointed to what he termed "division" between blacks and whites in North America. Johnsson wrote: "I have to question whether the current divided structures should continue indefinitely."[12] In a column published in the February 21, 2008, issue of the *Adventist Review*, columnist Frederick Russell wrote, "We will need at some point to disassemble the last symbols of our historical divide—racially segregated conferences in the United States."[13] By July 25, 2008, Russell's column was cited as the basis for an online petition[14] calling for the abolition of Regional and state conferences.[15] On September 29, 2009, Jan Paulsen, then president of the General Conference of Seventh-day Adventists, indicated, during a globally televised discussion with young adults from the Washington, DC, area, that he believed the thinking that produced Regional conferences (in 1944) is "no longer valid."[16] On January 16, 2010, Pastor Dwight Nelson of Andrews University preached a sermon, on Martin Luther King Weekend, in which he called Regional and state conferences "an amazing anomaly" and "separate but equal."[17]

Given the amount of discussion generated in internet chat rooms, periodicals, websites, and classrooms, it is helpful to initiate an open conversation that moves beyond the heat of assertions to the light of thoughtful consideration of biblical, theological, and missiological perspectives on some of the weightier questions raised by the continued presence of Regional conference structures in the NAD today. Questions related to this discussion of mission and structure include, but are not limited to, the following: Does the New Testament require or mandate an ideal organizational structure? Do passages such as John 17:21; Ephesians 2:14–18; or Galatians 3:27, 28 demand identicality of structure? What role, if any, do or should gender, race, culture, ethnicity, and nationality play in Christian mission and community building? Are "ethnic" structures de facto violations of Christian unity?

Should Regional conferences be considered evidence of "race-based organizational segregation" in the Seventh-day Adventist (SDA) Church? Should the creation of "ethnic" evangelism and congregations be discouraged or promoted? What is the biblical relationship between unity and diversity? And is the existence of state and Regional conferences "symbolic" of an ongoing divide between white and black Adventists in the United States?

We will begin our examination of these issues with a cursory look at examples of structure in the life of God's people in the Old and New Testaments. Next, we will summarize how mission and structure data in Scripture was understood by the early Adventist pioneers. Then we will examine how the contemporary Adventist Church understands the relationship between mission and structure. And finally, upon this biblical, theological, and missiological foundation, we will provide thoughtful responses to frequently asked questions regarding the existence of Regional conference structures.

Definition of terms

Affinity grouping—The practice of voluntarily affiliating around shared national, cultural, racial, linguistic, or gender commonalities.

African Americans—Persons of African descent residing in America (this definition includes Afro-Caribbean, Afro-Hispanic, and continental Africans in America).

Desegregation—The removal of legal barriers that restrict access to free and open use of public and private facilities as well as the voluntary association between willing parties.

Diversity—The plurality of cultures, races, gender, nationalities, and classes represented in the church. Its parameters are predetermined by the teachings of Scripture.

Ethnic—A group of people whose members identify with each other through a common heritage and are connected by shared cultural characteristics.

Integration—The voluntary affiliation and/or shared organizational membership of persons of different races, languages, nationalities, and sexes in common group settings.

Mission particularity—Mini- or macro-mission structures, organizations, and strategies dedicated to, directed at, and/or administered by specific people groups in North America.

Segregation—"The practice of restricting people to certain circumscribed areas of residence or to separate institutions and facilities on the basis of race or alleged race. Racial segregation provides a means of maintaining the economic advantages and higher social status of politically dominant races."[18]

Structure—Orderly, consensual arrangements formed by and within organizations to allocate human and financial resources, to delegate responsibility and flow of authority, to identify roles and relationships in an organization, and to ensure an appropriate, effective division of labor in the business or community.[19]

Unity—A shared commitment to a common purpose and a common set of beliefs and lifestyle practices. Biblical unity preserves the individuality of thought and action while focusing diversity on the person and work of Christ through the Holy Spirit. Unity's essential, dynamic, and equipoisal nature is described in John 17:21–23.[20]

Structure in the Old and New Testaments: A cursory survey

Why is Scripture important to a discussion of structure in the NAD? There are at least two reasons. First, as a Bible-believing community, Adventists actively and intentionally seek guidance from the teachings and principles of Scripture. Second, scriptural writers' articulation of the centrality of mission as God's action in the world provides a common focus for the discussion of the role of structure in the Adventist mission's implementation.

In the Old and New Testaments, minimal space is given to a

general discussion of organizational structure and its role in the mission of God's people. Within the pages of Scripture, an explicit presentation or discussion of structure rarely occurs. In fact, it appears that in the entire canon of Scripture, we find only a few examples of structure in the life of God's people—patriarchal (note Abraham's authority over his household in Genesis18:19; 24:4; 25:6; and Isaac's authority over his household in Genesis 26:30), judicial (see the book of Judges), prophetic (Moses, Aaron, etc.), Levitical/priestly, and monarchical.

In the New Testament, across the growth and development of the Christian church we find a variety of structures and models for the growing Christian movement—temple/synagogue, Messianic, apostolic/communal, representational (diaconate), and domestic/familial. The following chart highlights different dimensions of these varied governance and administrative structures.

Old Testament Governance/Administrative Structures

	Patriarchs	Prophetic	Adjudicative	Monarchical
Leaders	Abraham, Isaac, Jacob, etc.	Moses, 70 elders, etc.	Gideon, Deborah, Samson	Saul, Solomon, David
Decision-making Modality	Oracular	Oracular, delegated	Oracular	Personal/prophetic counsel
Resource Management	Patriarchs	Tribal leaders	Ruling judges	Kings

New Testament Governance/Administrative Structures

	Temple/ Synagogue	Messianic	Apostolic	Parental/ Familial[21]
Leaders	High priest/ priestly caste	Jesus Christ	Apostles, elders, deacons	Elders, overseers, household patrons (Romans 16)
Decision-Making Modality	Individualistic	Individual (Matthew 10:28, etc.)	Conciliar (Acts 15)	Elders/ house-church groups (1 Corinthians 16:19)
Resource Management	Priests	Disciples	Deacons (Acts 6)	Household patrons (Luke 12:42)

Due to its paucity, it is difficult to extrapolate much from this data. However, we can safely observe the following: (1) The Bible evinces a variety of structural arrangements related to the people of God in history. (2) We find no argument in the Bible for a particular structure that is used at all times and in all places. No single structure cuts across eras. (3) Organizational structure in Scripture expands, contracts, and/or adapts based on the scope and focus of the mission. (4) Structural arrangement that provides equitable representation is considered a vital dimension of service and witness (e.g., Acts 6). (5) Structures reflect continuity and discontinuity with the organizational structures of surrounding cultures, whether patriarchal or representative. (6) Organizational structures in Scripture reveal the following characteristics:

- They vary across time—from 3000 BC to AD 62.
- They vary across location—from Palestine to Rome.

- Flexibility differs based on the size of the community—Moses' millions to the house churches' small groups.
- Decision-making progresses from the Old to the New Testament, from patriarchal command-and-control decision-making to collaboration and consensus, from Abraham to the apostolic council (Acts 15).
- Material resource management moves from individual ownership to communal sharing, from Genesis to Acts.

Next, we look at how an understanding of Scripture influenced the approach of our Adventist pioneers to the issue of structure in the accomplishment of mission. We will see that they saw Scripture as a resource for principles, not prescriptions, in organizing the Advent movement.

Adventist pioneers' understanding of structure

Several Adventist scholars have studied the history of the Adventist pioneers' thinking and their journey on the issue of organizational structure.[22] In 2005, an important examination of SDA structure was also commissioned by the General Conference of Seventh-day Adventists.[23] It is not our purpose to fully rehearse the growth in the pioneers' attitude on issues of mission and structure. The dissertations and papers cited in the footnotes will provide the interested reader a detailed presentation of that history. However, we will cite highlights from SDA history to illustrate the background to today's Adventist approach to structure and mission.

According to SDA historian George Knight, "Seventh-day Adventist history represents the full spectrum on approaches to organization. The movement began aggressively anti-organizational, but today it is the most highly structured church in the history of Christianity."[24]

Knight's statement succinctly summarizes the pioneers' approach to the role of structure in the accomplishment of their mission. In the 1840s, some pioneers nurtured in the Millerite movement equated organization with "Babylon."[25] But as the church grew in the 1850s and '60s, it became clear to leaders such as James White that "gospel order" was needed.[26] Note White's somewhat humorous diatribe regarding those who believed that organizational structure would instantly or ultimately transform the Advent movement into Babylon:

> We are aware that these suggestions, will not meet the minds of all. Bro. Over-cautious will be frightened, and will be ready to warn his brethren to be careful and not venture out too far; while Bro. Confusion will cry out, "O, this looks just like Babylon! Following the fallen church!" Bro. Do-little will say, "The cause is the Lord's, and we had better leave it in his hands, he will take care of it." "Amen," says Love-this-world, Slothful, Selfish, and Stingy, "if God calls men to preach, let them go out and preach, he will take care of them, and those who believe their message;" while Korah, Dathan and Abiram are ready to rebel against those who feel the weight of the cause [e.g., James White], and who watch for souls as those who must give account, and raise the cry, "You take too much upon you."[27]

The Adventist pioneers believed that a commitment to effectiveness and efficiency in mission should be the primary driver of organizational form.

But organize they did. *They concluded that what the Bible did not prohibit, it permitted as long as the decision was vetted by counsel and common sense.* Notably, Barry Oliver pointed out that the early Adventist pioneers shunned prescriptive literalism when it came to developing an organizational structure and chose to appropriate biblical principles to inform organizational structure.[28] But even after that consensus was accepted, challenges occurred along the way.

Oliver points to a developing controversy in the 1890s.[29] This was the time when the Adventist Church had grown and was contemplating reorganization in 1903 to match the scope and focus of its mission. A. T. Jones and E. J. Waggoner, noted advocates for righteousness by faith at the 1888 Minneapolis General Conference, believed from their diligent study of the Scriptures that no human being should be called by the title "president."[30] In their ecclesiology, inasmuch as Christ was considered the head of the church, no human being deserved any titular designation such as "president." They believed that the title "president" would have assigned organizational leadership to a human being and thus would constitute a violation of New Testament ecclesiology. This radical ecclesiology threatened to split the church as it approached the 1903 General Conference reorganization. But Mrs. White did not support such biblically prescriptive reasoning. By January 1, 1863, and the organization of the Seventh-day Adventist General Conference, Ellen White and the pioneers had come to believe that the Bible did not contain rules for church structure but rather *principles* that should be applied to organizational design. The Adventist pioneers believed that a commitment to effectiveness and efficiency in mission should be the primary driver of organizational form.[31] This way of applying Scriptural principles in light of the obvious need for reorganization that was evident in the 1890s is what the pioneers sought to implement at the 1903 General Conference.

In summary, our SDA pioneers eventually concluded, notwithstanding considerable conflict over issues of organization, that *the Bible reveals principles rather than prescriptions for organization.*

Current Adventist perspectives on structure and mission

A few years ago, the work of Adventist scholars in researching and identifying these "pioneer principles" was incorporated into the work of a special Commission on Mission and Structure organized by the General Conference of Seventh-day Adventists. A report to the commission was voted by the Annual Council of the SDA Church October 15–17, 2007.[32] A complete version of the principles in the report, with elaboration, may be found on the General Conference website. In abbreviated form, these pioneer principles hold the following seven tenets:

1. "Organizational structure is necessary to fulfill the mission of the church."
2. "The Bible contains principles rather than prescriptions for organization."
3. "Commitment to mission is the primary determinant of structural form."
4. "Organizational structure must maintain a balance between centralization and decentralization, between control and empowerment."
5. "The design of organizational structure must provide for diversity while preserving unity."
6. "Flexibility in structure must not sacrifice unity and collective action."
7. "Changed circumstances warrant new or altered structures."[33]

Applied to our discussion of structure in the NAD, pioneer principle 1 acknowledges the indispensability of organization as a tool for the fulfillment of the church's mission. Organizational structure is created within community to define how human and financial resources will be deployed and how authority and responsibility for mission will be distributed. Pioneer principle 2 shows that of the numerous structures that have been observed in Scripture, *none* of them constitute a "blueprint" for the postcanonical church. Like the people of God in Scripture, the Adventist Church appropriates biblical principles *and* organizational elements from a variety of sources as long as the selected elements are considered compatible with the church's mission. This eclectic approach to organizational structure is adopted because the remnant ecclesiology of the Adventist Church is first *missional*.[34] Based on texts such as Matthew 5:13; 28:18–20; and Revelation 14:6–12, the Seventh-day Adventist Church's self-understanding is described in the following statement from Mrs. Ellen G. White: "The church is God's appointed agency for the salvation of men. It was organized for service, and its mission is to carry the gospel to the world. From the beginning it has been God's plan that through His church shall be reflected to the world His fullness and His sufficiency. The members of the church, those whom He has called out of darkness into His marvelous light, are to show forth His glory."[35]

Seventh-day Adventists, from their earliest reflections on structure, determined that mission should be the primary shaper of structural form. And the corollary followed closely on the heels of SDA mission—the primary shaper of mission would be Adventist eschatology. The Adventist pioneers' commitment to eschatology said to them and the growing Adventist community in the nineteenth century that "the time is at hand" and the world must be warned.[36] Adventist pioneers focused not on an idealized *nature* of the church but on the practical, effective *function* of the church. "Effectiveness of function" was the principle of organization followed by the pioneers.[37]

Though Adventists have only recently begun to explore a formal doctrine of ecclesiology,[38] the pioneers determined from their reading of the prophetic books of Daniel and Revelation that structures were needed to expedite the mission of the church. Thus, pioneer principle 3 in the report to the commission rightly asserts that mission determines structure. Here is precisely where we have not had a recent, transparent conversation around mission responsibility. May I submit that part of the reason we have such a rancorous discussion around Regional conferences in the NAD is because we have not had an open conversation about mission responsibility. Who in the NAD is responsible for reaching the 37.6 million African Americans in the NAD? Part of the reason we are in dispute is because we have not had an honest conversation around race and mission. The NAD has delegated mission primacy for reaching the 37.6 million African Americans in its territory to Regional conference ministries. The present structure, therefore, is the tool used to facilitate that mission to deliver the SDA message. Therefore, the following can be argued successfully: *Regional conferences are fully grounded in the mission particularity affirmed in pioneer principle 3—"Mission is the primary determinant of structural form."*

However, like the rest of the Seventh-day Adventist Church, Regional conferences are also committed to taking the gospel to the whole world. The entire church as the body of Christ is commissioned to carry the everlasting gospel to the whole world (Matthew 28:18–20; Revelation 14:6–12). While each people group will work to win a primary target population, each group should and must remain open to other people groups.[39] Mission segmentation means that the SDA Church should not expect every people group to identify the same mission targets or perform the same evangelistic task. Just as the hand's function is not to sneeze or chew or walk but to touch, hold, grab, and lift, so there will and should be diversity of focus and function in the execution of mission. In light of this Adventist missiology, the Regional conference structure appears to be a highly effective method of deploying human, financial, technological, and physical resources in maximizing the Adventist effort to reach the African American people group in the NAD with the SDA message.

Twenty-two years ago, Oliver noted that the church was slow in recognizing the need to respond in its structures to the diversity of the growing SDA Church. He wrote: "While Seventh-day Adventists have become one of the most ethnically diverse Christian denominations in the world, they remain not only in danger of failing to respond adequately to the changes that cultural diversity has brought, but they are even in peril of refusing to acknowledge that diversity necessitates structural adaptation."[40] Two decades after Oliver's groundbreaking research, it seems that his observation regarding the church's potential failure can no longer be considered absolute. Evidence for the difference in organizational outlook is reflected in SDA leadership's 2007 vote to receive the Report to the Commission at the Annual Council. Leaders at the 2007 Annual Council, as if in an affirmative response to Oliver's prescient criticism, voted to accept the commission report, which contained the following:

> Simply stated, there is need for flexibility in denominational structure—a flexibility that permits effective response to a particular set of conditions while at the same time maintaining the global values and identity of the Seventh-day Adventist Church. The reasons for increased flexibility rather than increased uniformity in structures and procedures may be summarized as follows:
>
> 1. Diversity of geographical environment. . . .
> 2. Differences in political, legal, and cultural environments. . . .
> 3. Geographical and cultural variations in receptivity to mission activities. . . .
> 4. Differentiation in local capacity, resources, and the need for coordinating and linking structures. . . .
> 5. The need for representation to be based on more than one model or classification of organization. . . .
> 6. Advances in technology open possibilities for new organizational patterns with increased efficiencies and effectiveness. . . .

What do these principles mean for structure in the NAD? Contrary to the calls for structural consolidation, Regional conference structures stand as an effective example of organizational flexibility— "a flexibility that permits effective response to a particular set of conditions while at the same time maintaining the global values and identity of the Seventh-day Adventist Church."[41]

Applied to regional structures, what is that set of conditions described in the above-referenced report?[42] First, the mission particularity of Regional conferences has been in response to the mission challenges of reaching the African American people group in North America. Missiologists generally use this term in reference to developing-world peoples. However, the term *people group* emphasizes the fact that African Americans have, from their arrival on American shores, constituted a subculture of the larger American culture.[43] Their unique history and culture have been a test of the civic conscience and foundational commitments of American democracy. Through Regional conference churches and leadership, the distinctive history and cultural perspective of African Americans has been penetrated by the cultural intelligence that drives Regional conference ministries. This mission has been supported by a structured and empowered stewardship of resources provided by Regional conference constituents.

Second, consistent with point 5, Regional conferences have provided leadership development opportunities that have benefited the larger Adventist Church and granted access and contribution to its larger councils. Part of what was being argued by the writers of the commission report referenced above has already been realized in the establishment of Regional conference structures.

In light of what we have seen in Scripture, Adventist history, and current reflection on Adventist structure and mission, we now turn to provide what we believe are thoughtful biblical, theological, and missiological answers that address the topics and questions that recently have been raised regarding the purpose and legitimacy of Regional conference structures.

Scriptural hermeneutics and structure

In looking at Regional conferences, there are some in our Adventist fellowship who interpret Scripture in a way that prohibits mission particularity in the name of unity. They ask questions such as: "Recently, our pastor preached a sermon in which he used a sentence from the prayer of Jesus, 'I pray that they may be one, even as we are one' (John 17:21). He said that Regional conferences and state conferences constitute division rather than unity in the North American Division. Does Scripture recommend a particular structure?"

In biblical interpretation, the science called *hermeneutics* guides the way we apply the ancient biblical text to current issues and situations.

No, Scripture does not recommend a particular structure. But to answer the question adequately, we must first establish a baseline for scriptural interpretation. In biblical interpretation, the science called *hermeneutics* guides the way we apply the ancient biblical text to current issues and situations. Hermeneutics is the method used by biblical scholars to interpret, understand, and apply biblical passages. The very first law of hermeneutics is to determine the specific subject under discussion in the biblical passage we are studying. If the subject under discussion in a biblical passage is not the same subject to which we are making a direct application of the text, then we are violating the biblical passage by using it as a *pretext* to support our personal perspectives and/or opinions. This technique is called *eisegesis*— reading into the passage a subject that the passage is not addressing. Now let's apply this hermeneutical law to John 17:21.

John 17:21 rests in the great priestly prayer of Jesus, that prayer offered just prior to His passion and crucifixion. Christ prays for the unity that His followers will need in order to survive His imminent passion and, later, the vicissitudes of history. His stated desire is for His followers to enjoy a unity akin to the oneness that He enjoys with His Father.[44] Because Jesus mentions His Father, it is clear that Trinitarian unity and its application to Christ's disciples is what Christ addresses in John 17:21. Christ is in the Father, and the Father is in Him. And the disciples are in Christ. Notice that the Father and Son, though individuated as personalities, enjoy oneness in purpose and mission. The issue of a specific structure in the early or later church is not under discussion in John 17:21–23.[45]

Biblical unity in John 17:21–23 forwards a profound oneness of mission and purpose, free from the divisive and ambitious strivings that would pit Christ's disciples against each other. Remember that the larger historical and biblical context of the prayer of John 17 includes John 13. That chapter describes the upper-room gathering where the divided and self-interested disciples would not wash one another's feet. However, the "glory" mentioned in the prayer of Christ is the glory that emanates from self-sacrificial service. Glory, self-sacrifice, is what Jesus prays that the world will see in the disciples' profound commitment to God and their unselfish service to each other.

When looked at carefully, John 17:21 actually makes the diversity-in-unity case most strongly. Marital unity, like Trinitarian unity, includes the same notion. The "two shall become one" of Genesis 2:24 does not mean that unity of purpose precludes individuation in expression. In fact, when one understands the depth of what Christ is praying for, one could argue that this very passage undermines the argument that the pastor thought John 17 supported. Singularity in organization or uniformity in thought is not required in this passage. In fact, the structure of the church is not even the subject of discussion in John 17:21–23.

Therefore, in order to apply this passage to a discussion on structure, the pastor had to preach John 17:21 through seven undeclared assumptions. First, the pastor had to see structure as the concern of Jesus' prayer. Second, the pastor had to assume that Regional and state structures violate biblical unity. Third, the pastor had to assume that mission particularity is divisive.[46] Fourth, the pastor had to assume that spiritual unity requires or implies structural singularity. Fifth, the pastor had to assume that only structural and/or congregational integration equals unity. Sixth, the pastor had to assume that Adventists move from biblical texts to direct prescriptions for structure. Seventh, the pastor had to assume that only integration and/or the multiracial congregational model of church life answers Christ's prayer.[47]

> Unity speaks to allegiance to a common faith, a common mission, and a common set of beliefs and values.

So what do we have here? Unity in John 17:21 points to the collective singularity of mission and purpose. According to *The Seventh-day Adventist Bible Commentary*, John 17:21 indicates that "there would be diversities of gifts (1 Cor. 12), but there was to be unity of spirit, objectives, and beliefs. There were to be no strivings for supremacy such as had recently plagued the Twelve (Luke 22:24–30). The unity springing from the blended lives of Christians would impress the world of the divine origin of the Christian church."[48]

The pastor exercised this opportunity to go beyond the text to misapply its teaching. In the technical study of preaching (*homiletics*), the pastor's use of the text to moralize about organizational structure is described by author Daniel Overdorf as "application heresy."[49]

Based on a definition of biblical unity, it may be argued that the NAD is united in mission. Regional and state conferences are united in the mission of declaring the Advent message of Revelation 14:6–12.[50] Unity speaks to allegiance to a common faith, a common mission, and a common set of beliefs and values. Regional conferences are no more divided from state conferences than state conferences are divided from each other. Regional conferences focus on a primary target population within a specific geographical region. Thus, the conference structure is simply a mechanism for deploying human and financial resources consistent with its assigned mission. So when we hear John 17:21 (or Ephesians 2:14–16 or Galatians 3:27, 28) cited as a basis for structural consolidation in the NAD, we know that such usages have no basis in responsible exegesis or in Seventh-day Adventist history.

The relationship between unity, diversity, and mission

Some believe that diversity is an aspect of Christian identity to be overcome in the light of Paul's statement, "There is neither Jew nor Greek, neither bond nor free, neither male nor female, but you are all one in Christ Jesus" (Galatians 3:27, 28).[51] This passage is seen as a call to a color-blind community. And they believe that those who speak affirmatively regarding culture, ethnicity, or gender are simply making excuses for division or "segregation" or maintenance of the status quo.

Their position prompts questions such as, "Aren't 'ethnic' structures (or congregations) de facto barriers to Christian mission in the NAD because they are 'segregated'?"

We place the word *ethnic* in quotes because ethnicity belongs to all people groups in the NAD, including Caucasians. The answer is no because these structures are not segregated (see the definition of *segregation*). Galatians 3:27, 28 is a call to a unified, not color-blind or class-blind or gender-blind, community. Race, class, culture, ethnicity, gender, age, and other aspects of diversity are redeemed and presented in the New Testament by Paul not as barriers but as resources for mission.[52] Many, if not most, Christians have been taught that race, class, and ethnicity are dimensions of identity that must be left behind after becoming a Christian. But biblical unity does not create a diversity-blind community or mission. In 1 Corinthians 9:18–24, a passage in which Paul discusses the missional use of redeemed cultural and ethnic particularity, the apostle says to the Corinthian community, "To the Jew, I became as a Jew . . . to *win* the Jews" (verse 20, NRSV; emphasis added). Here Paul—who also said to the Galatians, who were inappropriately using ethnicity, class, and gender to establish and advance cultural and religious superiority, "There is neither Jew, nor Greek" (Galatians 3:28, KJV)—now affirms to the Corinthians that his ethnicity did not disappear upon becoming a Christian. His pre-Christian history, culture, race, class, and other attributes were transformed into a mission-usable resource that he deployed to reach other Jews with the saving gospel of Jesus Christ. In other words, Paul established points of contact that were rooted in important aspects of the ethnic and cultural identity that he shared with other Jewish persons. By this means, Paul was able to speak the cultural language of his people.

Based on Paul's missiology, Japanese, Ghanaian, Russian, Hispanic (i.e., Latino), Korean, African American, Filipino, Euro-American, and a host of other ethnic congregations in the NAD stand as examples of believers who resource important aspects of their racial, cultural, and ethnic identities to advance Adventist mission. These believers know that the grace of God, which is no respecter of persons, is a grace that radiates from all people to all people and through all people (remember Acts 10:34–36). These "ethnic" congregations are committed to meeting people groups in North America in the language, folkways, and cultural idioms that speak the gospel most deeply to their communities of origin.[53] More important, ethnic congregations are open and accessible to any believer who wishes to visit or join. A "color-blind" missiology would require that racial, ethnic, and national particularity in mission be eliminated. According to the *Encyclopaedia Britannica Online*, racial segregation is the "practice of restricting people to certain circumscribed areas of residence or to separate institutions and facilities on the basis of race or alleged race. Racial segregation provides a means of maintaining the economic advantages and higher social status of the politically dominant group."[54] Thus, no Adventist congregation in the NAD is segregated. Adventist congregations reflect missional particularity.

In this conversation, we appeal to all, regardless of one's position on this matter, let us agree that we will be charitable in the framing of this discussion. We note that critics of Regional conferences are increasingly misusing some of the most polarizing terms from the Jim Crow era of American history. Terms such as *segregation* and *separate but equal* are recently being preached from our pulpits to describe the NAD structure. Leaders are being accused of being power hungry, racist, or separatist. Such careless and reckless brandishing of these volatile terms is misleading, uninformed, and divisive.[55] The Adventist Church does not support segregation. Every Seventh-day Adventist in America is free to attend and/or join any Adventist congregation in North America if that Adventist is a member in "regular standing" in his or her local church.

Structure and SDA Church history

Some are embarrassed by the racial history of the Adventist Church that gave birth to Regional conferences. They believe that the refusal of the church to accept black members' requests for integration in 1944 was wrong and that decision must now be reversed to reflect societal progress on racial issues. They ask such questions as: "Are not Regional conferences a reminder of an embarrassing failure in SDA history?"

On one hand, the answer is yes. The regretful history of the Adventist Church's treatment of blacks between 1890 and 1965 is well documented. "That conflictual history," according to some, "is the reason that we should disband regional conferences now that the church and society have changed so drastically since 1944." Is it not time that we eliminate "a racially defined organizational structure?" they ask.[56]

On the other hand, we say no because history does not have to be perfect to be purposeful. To reason only from the historical occurrences of 1944 and that era is to limit our view of history to horizontal cause and effect. However, Ellen White articulates a vertical view of history that is quite illuminative. She wrote: "Behind, above, and through all the play and counterplay of human interests and power and passions, [stand] the agencies of the all-merciful One, silently, patiently working out the counsels of His own will."[57]

Another oft-quoted statement is, "In reviewing our past history, having traveled over every step of advance to our present standing, I can say, Praise God! As I see what the Lord has wrought, I am filled with astonishment, and with confidence in Christ as leader. We have nothing to fear for the future, except as we shall forget the way the Lord has led us, and His teaching in our past history."[58]

Her view is that the hand of God is revealed in the "advance to our present standing." Her conclusion also means—human interests, power, and passion notwithstanding—history does not have to be perfect to be purposeful!

Several significant breakthroughs in Adventist progress and understanding grew out of the vortex of conflictual history among leaders of the movement. Examples include the testy showdown over the nature of salvation between G. I. Butler and Uriah Smith, on one side of the righteousness-by-faith issue, and A. T. Jones and E. J. Waggoner, on the other, at the 1888 Minneapolis General Conference. This is a notable example of a historical conflict that yielded significant progress for the theological development of our doctrine of salvation.[59] Another example is the historical conflict between Ellen G. White and the leadership of the Battle Creek Sanitarium and J. H. Kellogg in the 1890s over the nature of Adventist health care and church authority. This conflict yielded clearer and more distinct understandings of our mission in health care and its relationship to the ecclesiastical side of our organization.[60] Another example is the disagreement between the Southern California Conference and John Burden over whether to purchase Loma Linda in 1904 when the conference president instructed Burden not to proceed with the purchase—while Ellen G. White said to go forward.[61] Other examples from SDA history could be cited. But as we review that history, we see that greater glory of God was born from the womb of historical conflict.

> Over and above his brothers' inadequate treatment, Joseph saw the larger, purposeful will of God being accomplished.

The life of Old Testament Joseph illustrates this vertical "superventionist" view of history, which is explicated in Ellen G. White's writings. In Genesis 45:5, Joseph, when confronting his frightened brothers over their mistreatment of him, said to them, "And now do not be distressed or angry with yourselves because you sold me here, for God sent me before you to preserve life" (ESV). Their view of history was horizontal. But Joseph had a vertical interpretation of that painful history. "You sold me . . . but God sent me" said Joseph. In other words, God did not contravene in this case, He supervened. Over and above his brothers' inadequate treatment, Joseph saw the larger, purposeful will of God being accomplished. Reading God's purposeful will said to Joseph, the victim of his brothers' treachery, that God had an overarching redemptive purpose in his maltreatment. It was God's purpose that through Joseph's horrid history, a greater glory would be manifested on behalf of the suffering Hebrew people. In the New Testament, a similar assessment of human activity is also contained in the Gamaliel principle—if the plan is of man, it will fail. If the plan is of God, you will not be able to stop it (see Acts 5:38, 39).

Similarly, it is an established fact that in 1944, in the wake of the

Lucy Byard incident at Washington Sanitarium, African Americans requested the full integration of all facilities and structures of the Seventh-day Adventist Church in North America.[62] In response, the General Conference Spring Council of April 8–15, 1944, voted to organize Regional conferences "where the colored constituency is . . . sufficiently large, and where financial income and territory warrant."[63] In 1945, Lake Region was organized. And by December 1945, four conferences were organized for the Negro (colored) people, with four more to be organized by 1951. Ironically, from the time African Americans were given conferences to operate, the Adventist work among African Americans expanded dramatically during the twentieth century.

Now we raise a question that to moderns will sound like social heresy: In the context of Adventist missiology, suppose integration would have hindered the embryonic black work? Remember, it was integration that hindered God's work during Edson White's mission activities around the turn of the century. The segregationist context was not substantially different in 1944 than in 1909. In 1944, full-scale integration was still an extremely liberal political idea in racially conservative America.[64] Today, we assume that if the answer to the request for integration had been yes, the tolerance we know today would have simply been replicated in 1944.[65] Such a conclusion raises the question of whether we fully appreciate the racial animus and antipathy that pervaded relations between blacks and whites in the 1940s in America. In criticizing the General Conference leadership of that era, we sometimes overlook the fact that twenty-first-century outlooks on race are the cumulative result of fifty years of social upheaval around issues regarding race in America.[66] But racial intolerance in 1944, prior to the Civil Rights movement of the '50s and '60s, the social experimentation of the '70s, and the tolerance and diversity movements of the '80s and '90s, was aggressively assimilationist,[67] committedly colonialist, and deeply embedded in the outlooks and institutions of America, including the Seventh-day Adventist Church. Accession to the 1944 request for integration of structure, in such a fiercely unwelcoming racial environment, might have driven more leaders than Lewis C. Sheafe[68] and James K. Humphrey[69] out of the Adventist Church. SDA historians and scholars writing about this period consistently assume that integration in 1944 would have been the best missional decision for the future of black work.[70] These assumptions explain why some consider Regional conferences "God's non-ideal plan."[71]

But this view not only minimizes the historical context of 1944 but also is predicated on the assumption that, in a hierarchy of values, integration should be the highest value and should have been implemented at all costs.[72] But we submit that such a position is driven by a view of integration that somehow sees interracial affiliation as a moral imperative.[73] Interestingly, if Ellen G. White had been similarly ideological in her view of integration, she would have insisted at the turn of the century that whites and blacks *must* worship together, even if it would be at the cost of believers' lives. She could have quoted any of a number of texts to support a morally grounded position (e.g. Acts 5:1–10; Hebrews 12:14, 15 or Acts 17:26, He "hath made of one blood all nations" [KJV]). But Ellen White was not an integrationist ideologue who insisted that the future vision of the *eschaton* be precisely replicated in our present situation. In this regard, Mrs. White would be classified today as a missional contextualist.[74] One need only read her handling of the mission issues related to the "color line" in the nineteenth century to observe her mindset.[75] Before "situational leadership" would be posited some sixty years later, Ellen White demonstrated a case-based approach to resolving mission issues. Based on her counsel to the Southern field, she believed that our mission must interface effectively with the local, cultural, social, and historical context.[76] While in her early statements she initially supported equality at Creation and in cross-racial affiliation, she was not slavishly bound to that support.[77] The moral implications of this adjustment in Ellen White's counsel on the relationship between the races have gone unnoticed by scholars. For her, effective SDA mission was both practically and contextually responsive.[78]

Second, Adventist writers about this period consistently fail to show that Regional conferences were also established for missional purposes.[79] Like historically black colleges and universities in America (e.g., Oakwood University), Regional conferences were responses to exclusion. However, they were much more than that. A careful reading of the documents chronicling their founding shows that General Conference leadership in 1944 also believed that blacks could better organize, manage, and execute SDA mission to black America. What is consistently neglected in the discussion of the NAD structure is the accompanying second track of missiological motivation behind the establishment of Regional conferences.[80] This is not to imply that GC leaders were guiltless. They were not. It is clear that they chose the path of least resistance on the social front. But, as time passed, the legal and social context of segregation disappeared over the next thirty years, but the missiological necessity for Regional conferences did not. The critics of Regional conference structures, in their efforts to invalidate or delegitimize them, cite only the segregationist history and failure of then leaders. They fail to cite the accompanying and stated missiological rationale for the creation of the structures. Therefore, it does not follow that since the context of segregation has ended, the structures must automatically end also. Regardless of the motives and/or mistakes of our Adventist forefathers, Regional conferences continued as mission-particularized structures created for the missional purpose of empowering black leaders to evangelize America's black peoples.[81] And as asserted earlier, history did not have to be perfect to be purposeful.

Regional structures and segregation

Some believe that Regional and state conferences are carryovers from pre–civil rights era segregation. This perspective prompts questions similar to the following: "Don't Regional conferences constitute 'race-based organizational segregation'?"

The answer is no.[82] In fact, use of this terminology is erroneous, volatile, and misleading. No one who understands what segregation entailed in the Jim Crow South would consider the Adventist Church in the NAD segregated. Any member can join any church. Interracial marriage is not prohibited. Every institution owned and operated by the Adventist Church is available to all of its members.

Thus, what some call "segregation" overlooks the missiological imperative of mission particularity. Mission particularity means that we organize at the structural level to reach specific target populations. Ironically, unless one's moral position insists that all local churches be integrated and that ethnic congregations (such as Latino, Anglo, Ghanaian, or Japanese) be eliminated, it is logically inexplicable to support the organization of "ethnic" congregations while viewing the organization of those same congregations into conferences as a form of segregation. But we have yet to read one description of the various "ethnic" structures in the NAD (whether congregations, departments, or ministries) that is labeled "segregated."

Further, a reasonable question follows: if Regional conferences (as examples of mission particularity) are considered participants in "race-based organizational segregation," what prevents us from considering women's ministries departments to be "gender-based organizational segregation"? Why should we not consider Christian Record Braille as "disability-based organizational segregation"? Why should we not consider Korean camp meetings as evidence of "nationality-based organizational segregation"? And should we not consider the Adventist Youth Department "age-based organizational segregation"? The fact is that each of these organizational units, and that includes Regional conferences, reflects mission particularity.

So why do we sometimes hear and read such heated criticism of the NAD for its persistent support for the ministries of Regional conferences? One of the reasons Regional conference structures have been labeled as "race-based organizational segregation" is because of the historical sensitivity in the United States around the subject of race.[83] In the NAD, race is an unfinished conversation. One cannot discuss race in the history of America without arousing the discomfort that de jure and de facto racism has caused in American society since the founding of the country.[84] Discussions of race call issues such as power, privilege, access, equality, and control into question.[85] Conservative Christians generally do not see themselves as responsible, party to, or practitioners of discrimination. [86] Many conservative Christians find it difficult to converse publicly about these issues. In 1999, the NAD convened its first summit on race. The announced plan was to convene a follow-up summit to build on the recommendations from the first summit. To the disappointment of many, requests to convene the follow-up summit have been consistently denied.

A second reason that Regional conference structures have come under criticism is that some see them as a reminder of painful racial history in America. Many wish that discussions of that history would just "go away." They read into that difficult history a continuing and unresolved hostility between blacks and whites in the NAD, "a symbol of the historic divide" between the races. These speakers and writers call for "racial reconciliation," which, in their view, will be evidenced in the dissolution of Regional conferences and the creation of new structures. Their vision of reconciliation results in structural consolidation.

Observation indicates that some who wish to abolish Regional conferences often display a limited knowledge of the history of how Regional conferences were born. Others, who have some fluency regarding this period of SDA history, consistently read that history only horizontally, whereas this analysis puts forward a vertical reading of that same history. As mentioned previously, Joseph's vision of God's providential purpose (Genesis 45:1–8) frames our view of this period of SDA history. And as has been pointed out earlier, despite the difficult history of African Americans in the Adventist Church from 1890 to 1945, God provided a "better way." That way came in stages across the first seven decades of the twentieth century. First, in 1909, the organizing of the Negro Department put in place a structured responsibility of mission to black people. Though the first three leaders were white, the organization, at the prompting of J. K. Humphrey, incorporated mission to blacks into the organized structure of the church.[87] Second, Regional conferences were organized in 1944 through a corporate church decision to support mission to black America in the form of structural empowerment that entrusted responsibility and resources to African Americans. The 1944 decision meant the colonial models for administering the mission to blacks in America had been rejected in favor of the complete empowerment of black leadership. Third, in 1962, the equal rights movements of the 1950s and '60s were paralleled by civil rights activism within the Adventist Church by the Laymen's Leadership Conference.[88] This group of Negro professionals demanded and enabled the free and open association of whites and blacks in voluntary local church worship and fellowship, equal access to all SDA-owned institutions, and representation at every level of church structure. Their effort culminated in the 1965 declaration of equal rights by SDA leaders. These "better way" decisions for African American empowerment represented a break with other colonially structured models. These decisions drove dramatic growth in the evangelistic accessions to the SDA church.

A third reason that Regional conference structures have come under criticism is the obvious misunderstanding of segregation, desegregation, and integration. The critics of Regional conferences cited in this study wrongly assume that the opposite of segregation is integration. But the opposite of segregation is not integration but desegregation. Segregation in the history of America was coercive and legal in its enforcement. Desegregation was the reversal of those laws of enforced discrimination. Desegregation does not require integration; rather, it removes the legal barriers that prohibit integration.

The fact of the matter is that the SDA Church does not support or practice segregation. Here is where greater precision must be requested in our NAD discourse. Let us not confuse segregation with affinity grouping.[89] Affinity grouping in the Adventist community is not segregation but voluntary affiliation. Affinities based on national, racial, cultural, and ethnic similarities strengthen the overall body of Christ, rather than weaken it—when these affinities become resources for mission. Division is avoided as long as the diversity of the body stays united in its mission on behalf of the church and is inclusive of those who want to unite with its fellowship. If, and when, racial, cultural, ethnic, and gender groups individuate around missional purpose, and such individuation is viewed as divisive in the NAD, then the division's only recourse is to ban the formation of "ethnic" congregations, dissolve men's and women's ministry departments, disallow Korean, Chinese, Ghanaian, Filipino, or Latino camp meetings, and call for homogeneity and uniformity in the name of unity.

But such a posture would be a gross violation of the organic unity and diversity dynamic that is embedded in our shared ecclesiastical life. New Testament theologian Thomas R. Schreiner writes, "The body is one and yet has many different members; the variety of members does not nullify the fact that there is one body. . . . [But] by definition, the one body is also characterized by diversity (1 Cor. 12:14), for bodies are made up of many members."[90]

A final reason that Regional conferences have come under criticism recently is because many in the NAD are deeply concerned about efficiency and duplication of services during a time of financial recession. However, the question of duplication of services seems valid only to the extent that Regional conferences share duplicate target populations with other entities.

Ellen G. White: Racial idealist or mission realist?

Many recall a well-known statement made by Ellen G. White that suggests a temporary accommodation in the separation between blacks and whites. This recollection prompts questions similar to the following: "Did not Mrs. White anticipate a 'better way' at the turn of the century?"[91]

The statement concerns the efforts to integrate congregations in the racially charged Southern United States by Adventist workers and ministers in the southern field. It was written in 1909. Here is the statement, as penned by Mrs. White: "Let the colored believers be provided with neat, tasteful houses of worship. Let them be shown that this is done not to exclude them from worshiping with white people, because they are black, but in order that the progress of the truth may be advanced. Let them understand that this plan is to be followed until the Lord shows us a better way."[92]

In 1891 Mrs. White left for Australia, but she never forgot her burden for the "colored people" in the South. From Australia, she sent a string of testimonies to workers in the Southern field. Her son, Edson White, led a very high-profile missionary initiative to the Negroes of the South. Partly inspired by Mrs. White's famous March 21, 1891, sermon to the twenty-ninth General Conference Session, "Our Duty to the Colored People,"[93] Edson charged ahead with ministry to the blacks of the South, beginning in the Mississippi delta.

Edson White's vision for ministry led him to believe that the Adventist message called for the blacks and whites to worship together. But Ronald Graybill, SDA historian on Ellen White and the race relations of the period between 1895 and 1909, asserted that the acceptance of segregation came to be the American way. The years 1890 through 1920 are known as a period of lynching, disenfranchisement, riots, and terrorist violence directed toward the Negro population. In this environment, social mixing of the black and white races in the South was found to be dangerous and discouraged by Mrs. White.[94] Interestingly, Ellen White saw no hypocrisy in believing in a doctrine of racial equality but respecting social conventions where disregarding them would jeopardize the progress of the mission among the colored believers.[95]

It is important to note that the emphasis of Mrs. White's 1909 "better way" statement is focused on the question of methodology; on the best way to make the greatest progress among both colored and white believers in the South in the face of overwhelming white racism. Social mixing of blacks and whites threatened the success of the Adventist message with both blacks and whites in the Southern field.[96] At the turn of the century, Mrs. White feared that if social mixing of the races continued during this period, colored believers and white workers might lose not only their livelihoods but also their lives.[97] The "better way" statement was written thirty-five years before Regional conferences were founded. Thus, Mrs. White's comment could not be in reference to the transience of Regional conferences. The statement raises the question of what the best way was to prosecute mission to the colored people within the overall Adventist mission to black

Ellen White took quite seriously the social context and challenges facing Adventist ministry to black America. Her comments show that she was not a dogmatic idealist but a practical realist.

America. Ellen White took quite seriously the social context and challenges facing Adventist ministry to black America. Her comments show that she was not a dogmatic idealist but a practical realist. She shunned dichotomous thinking on the issue, choosing rather to hold both notions in tension—blacks are equal to whites, but mission must be contextualized if it is to be effective. In this case, according to Ellen G. White, nothing should be done that would stir up hostility.[98] Methodologically, she believed that God would show a "better way" to advance mission among colored believers.

We submit that the "better way" arrived in three GC leadership decisions that occurred in the twentieth century: (1) The establishment of the Negro Department in 1909 (a quarter century before the formation of the first Regional conference) provided a structural home for directing the mission to colored members in America. The Negro Department elevated the church's mission to the colored people from an ad hoc, hortatory effort to one granting the mission fully institutionalized status. (2) With the 1944 creation of Regional conferences, and the accompanying indigenization of leadership, displacement of colonial-style operation of the work created a pipeline for future African American leadership development. Mission particularity replaced colonial models for mission to the Negro. (3) The work of the Layman's Leadership Conference during the civil rights movement of the 1950s and '60s enabled the free association of the races and allowed open fellowship of blacks and whites. This action took care of the socially forced "separation" between blacks and whites referenced in Mrs. White's 1909 statement. Thus the SDA church has provided organizational support for mission to black America (1909), for empowerment of native and immigrant black leaders within the structure of the NAD for the purpose of evangelizing the black peoples of America (1944), and voluntary interracial fellowship in our churches (1962–1965). The dramatic mission growth that has occurred among African Americans in the wake of each of these decisions is evident. The "better way" is here.

"Race-based" structures and witness

Some say that the Adventist Church in the NAD appears to be divided around race. They believe that the way to signal unity is to dismantle Regional conferences or to dissolve both Regional and state conferences and create one conference. Their concern results in questions such as the following: "If we have Regional and state conference structures, does it reflect a poor witness to the non-Adventist world?"

No. Our conference structures are constructs of the collective mind of the SDA organization. As such, these structures are not tangible but mental schemas represented in constitutions and territories that allow for the allocation of human and financial resources, as well as the working delegation of authority and responsibility for mission. For instance, when one lands at Dulles or Reagan airports in Washington, DC, no one is able to disembark from his/her flight, look over Washington, DC, and say, "The Allegheny East Conference begins here, and Potomac Conference starts there."

On the other hand, after landing, one is able to look around and say, "Dupont Park Church stands here, and Capital Memorial Church sits over there." Why? Because local congregations are the places where visible, tangible, witness is lived out. Local congregations gather in communities to worship, to fellowship, and to minister to each other and their communities. As Elder Charles Bradford, former president of the NAD, was fond of saying, "All ministry is local."[99] What communities experience (or do not experience) is the life of local congregations of believers. Thus, if mission particularity hurts the witness of the church, then the witness of the church is hurt every Sabbath when its mostly homogenous congregations gather in the cities and suburbs. It is unfair to attribute poor witness to what people cannot see (i.e., conference structures) by overlooking what communities see every Sabbath in our local congregations!

Regional conferences and interracial fellowship

Some who object to the existence of Regional conferences are genuinely concerned about how God's people can enjoy fellowship and regular association with each other if structurally they are kept apart. They ask questions similar to the following: "Does having state and Regional conferences keep the church in the NAD 'separated'?"

No. One way to answer this question is to compare fellowship patterns within the NAD unions where Regional conferences do not exist with unions where they do exist. In the North Pacific Union (NPUC), Pacific Union (PUC), and Canadian Union (CUC), there are no Regional conferences. Yet the same patterns of affinity grouping in Hispanic, Asian, Caucasian, and African American churches seen in the eastern United States are also seen in NPUC, PUC, and CUC. Something far deeper than structure is keeping churches particularized. It is cultural affinity—that powerful glue that gives groups their markers of identity, influences patterns of socialization, and causes persons to hold membership in a distinctive group. After conversion, this normal human dynamic is sanctified, not abolished; enlisted, not eliminated as an evangelistic resource in the mission of the church.[100]

One failure in this discussion on structure appears to be an ideological blind spot that overlooks the biblical use of diversities (such as culture, history, or experience) as resources for advancing mission. What we are hearing is an insistence that diversity identities should be ignored (color-blindness) in Christian mission and community building. But "color-blindness" is a distinctively nonmissional commitment that decontextualizes mission activity by replacing it with Americanized, melting-pot idealism.

Regional conferences and the twenty-first century

With the election in 2008 of Senator Barack Obama to the presidency of the United States, some believe that America's historical vision of itself as a melting pot was realized. In their judgment (especially among some of our younger, post–civil rights–oriented members), America is a post-racial society. Therefore, they wonder, how can we operate a race-based organization in the twenty-first century? They ask, "Since we are living in a post-racial society, why do we operate structures that are race-based?"

First, no current reading of the research literature on race in America could convincingly lead to the conclusion that the country or our world is "post-racial." *Post-racial* is a term popularized by political pundits. Like many phrases du jour, *post-racial* means different things to different people. The term has been used to describe an era when race no longer matters in public discourse and decision making. It can mean that society, in general, is oblivious to racial differences. For some, it means a society in which people's abilities are more important than their race. For others, *post-racial* anticipates a society where we are no longer defined by racial categories. If America is post-racial, such color-blindness has not shown up in any significant research on how race affects quality of life. In fact, data from research into health-care disparities points to exactly the opposite—America is anything but post-racial.[101]

Second, because America is a pluralistic society, race- and gender-specific organizations operate consistently in America. For example, in America, we have the American Medical Association, National Medical Association, Historically Black Colleges and Universities, National Hispanic Caucus, National Council of Hispanic Women, National Council of Negro Women, Advancing Women in Leadership, National Association for the Advancement of Colored People, Asian American Cancer Association, Asian and Pacific Islander Wellness Association, Korean American Professional Society, Network of Indian Professionals, South Asian Women's Leadership Forum, Network of South Asian Professionals, and the list could go on. In this discussion of Regional conferences, some speak as if ethnic- and race-specific organizations do not exist in America and unwittingly imply that the Adventist Church is the only organization in America with particularized structures. Such is obviously not the case. Race-based organizations that are inclusive and achieve the mission of the parent organization are perfectly acceptable forms of organizational life.

Third, who expropriated the authority to declare that anything "race-based" is, by definition, un-Christian? In US politics, "race-based" has come to be associated with racial discrimination or prejudice or social remedies. And because each of these is so politically polarizing, some reflexively associate the idea of "race-based" with these negative realities. However, from a missional perspective, race-based is no different from gender-based or language-based or nationality-based or culture-based tactics used to reach various people groups. Like other demographic categories, race has been and continues to be a crucial taxonomic category of population classification in North America.

Adventists operate Regional conferences because, as a church, we have seen the evidence that these structures are a proven and effective tool to equip, and empower those on the front lines in the mission of reaching the 37.6 million African Americans living in the United States. Regional conferences are the empowered organizational extensions of operating African American churches. Conference status is nothing more and nothing less than an efficient way of organizing black churches for mission. While in our general US society, "race-based" can imply exclusionary practices, such is not the case with Regional conferences. While holding a primary target population, Regional conferences, consistent with their original design, welcome a growing cadre of nonblack congregations who voluntarily choose Regional conferences because they find the historic evangelism emphasis embedded in the African American Adventist culture compatible with their own sense of mission to their primary people groups.

Duplication of services and Regional conferences

Some are concerned about the financial impact of operating over-lapping structures in the seven unions in the NAD where state and Regional conferences exist. They ask whether the church can afford the luxury of duplicate efforts: "Is not having Regional and state conferences in the NAD a duplication of services?"

No. Having two structures in a geographic region is no more duplication of services than having two or ten churches in the same city is a duplication of services. Duplication of services occurs only where we have a *duplication of mission*. If Regional and state conferences targeted the same people group as their target popula-tion, then we would have a duplication of services. What we have is similar infrastructure with a differentiated mission focus. We call that mission particularity, and mission particularity is what the constituencies of Regional conferences support with $200 million in tithes and multiplied millions more in offerings for mission.

Ellen G. White and nationalism

Some read Ellen White's prohibition of the formation of confer-ences around nationality[102] as a basis for prohibiting the formation of Regional conferences. They wonder about such questions as the following: "If Ellen G. White refused to support the creation of German and Scandinavian conferences in 1905, would she not refuse to support Regional conferences in 1944?"

This question raises the issue of the hermeneutics of interpreting Ellen White. The answer to the question is that we cannot specu-late about what she would do on the basis of her counsel in one case unless we can verify that the circumstances of the known case mirror those of another case. A second reason that we cannot use this approach is because it is also dangerous to take a statement from Mrs. White and make it an absolute projection of what she would do in another circumstance.

But did not Mrs. White insist in 1905 that all people work across national and racial lines? It might appear that way if we read selectively. But this is exactly the opposite of what she counseled in the case of whites and blacks in the same period. She wrote in 1909: "Instead of wondering whether they are not fitted to labor for white people, let our colored brethren and sisters devote themselves to missionary work among the colored people."[103]

Consider another example. In 1891, Mrs. White wrote that blacks and whites should worship together because a terrible wrong had been done to the colored people and the church of God should make no distinction.[104] But are we justified in seeing that statement as an absolute, stand-alone pronouncement and concluding that regardless of the circumstances, Ellen White intended for whites and blacks to worship together in 1891 and going forward? No. That position faces a problem! Eighteen years later, in 1909, she wrote that blacks and whites should worship *separately.*[105] Which counsel was right? Ellen White's principle regarding counsel was consistent. She explained the principle she used in approaching various situations: "But while we present methods of work, we cannot lay out an undeviating line in which everyone shall move, for circumstances alter cases."[106] It is hermeneutically inappropriate to conclude that the exact conditions present in 1905 were the same in 1944 and that, therefore, because Mrs. White prohibited a certain action in 1905, she would automatically prohibit it in 1944.

In 1901, under the leadership of General Conference president Arthur G. Daniells, the General Conference undertook a major reorganization of the Adventist Church. At that session, leaders of the German work proposed that each of the unions in America designate a leader to coordinate the work among the growing German immigrant population of America. After some discussion, the request was granted. On its heels came a request from the Scandinavians. That motion was accepted without discussion.[107]

What were the pertinent circumstances under which the Germans and Scandinavians were requesting conferences? We do not know much about the history external to the testimony, but hints are present in what Mrs. White sanctions and/or rebukes in this case. Content analysis of the testimony reveals that Mrs. White saw a violation of the John 17:21 unity paradigm for God's church. In the German-Scandinavian case, Mrs. White saw a spirit of self-magnification that would violate the unity of John 17:21. She used words such as "magnify themselves"[108] and "ambitious propositions."[109] Apparently what Mrs. White saw behind the proposal was a divisive and self-seeking ethnocentrism and nationalism veiled in outward mission mindedness but that would eventually "create dissension."[110] Her answer to this spirit was the self-sacrificial mutuality described in the prayer of Christ in John 17—"We are to be subject to one another" she said. She declared that "each nationality should labor earnestly for every other nationality."[111] Mrs. White uses John 17:21 to condemn the striving and nationalistic self-assertion that short-circuited mutuality and mission. A conference formed under such motivations would have sown divisiveness in the church and built up walls of nationalistic division. Mrs. White saw that this proposal would not, in her words, "advance the interests of the work among the various nationalities."[112]

Regional conferences and racial and ethnic reconciliation

Some of our members observe other Christian denominations participating in racial reconciliation conferences and ask: "According to Ephesians 2:14–16 and Galatians 3:26–28, are not believers from every ethnicity, race, class, gender, and nationality called on to reconcile and unite as one? And is not the maintenance of Regional conferences and state conferences a violation of the unity announced in these passages?"

Yes, believers are called to live in harmony with one another. And where there has been hostility (as seen in Ephesians 2:14–16), Christ's reconciling activity is viewed as the basis for a new humanity—one that is reconciled to God and reconciled to people formerly considered antagonists or outcasts. However, once again, we must ask: On what basis and authority is affinity grouping considered antagonism?

In order to conclude that people groupings violate the teachings of these passages, one must judge Ghanaian churches as alienated from Korean churches, Anglo churches as alienated from Latino churches, Filipino churches as hostile to African American churches, and so on. But affinity groupings are not de facto, segregation, alienation, or hostility. The fact that Adventist churches operate from a common set of fundamental beliefs; common operational policies; common financial policies; and, most important, a common mission indicates that the unity desired for the congregations in the NAD already exists. For greater interracial fellowship at the local level, local pastors are free to affiliate, trade pulpits, plan and launch shared mission events, and create joint worship experiences across racial lines as frequently as these are desired.

At the structural level, the answer to the question is no. Regional and state conferences are violations of unity only if hostility, acrimony, or exclusivity toward others dominates conference culture. As with other units of SDA organization, Regional and state conferences are each committed to the single mission of the Adventist Church. Division would mean that Regional and state conferences are working at cross purposes with each other. Further, to use these passages to prescribe a particular organizational structure is an example of the "application heresy" referenced earlier.

Change or mission?

There are many who feel that the need for a change is overdue. How should we go about changing? Should it start from the top or come up from the bottom? Some are asking: "When will we change?"

We find that a careful, thoughtful, and prayerful examination of the relationship between mission and structure and an exegetically responsible reading of Scripture, along with careful missiological analysis, reveal that there are no theologically supportable objections to mission particularity expressed in the form of Regional conference structures. "Mission is the determinant of structural form." We have also demonstrated that no biblical definition of unity is violated by mission particularity. Clearly the push toward consolidation is not driven by an informed understanding of missiology. Apparently, the conversation that we need to explore is the relationship between unity and diversity, for scripturally, the presence of diversity does not equal disunity.

One reason this issue is so sensitive is that it turns on our ability or inability to discuss race. For instance, on the one hand, we hear a call to dismantle mission-particularized structures; but rarely does anyone making the demand discuss the impact of "white flight" in the NAD. Yet, we know that once predominately white congregations have black memberships that exceed 25 percent,[113] Caucasians begin to move out of those congregations, thus abandoning them to members of color. This leads to crucial questions for this discussion: Would the rush by some to mandate integration adversely affect the "white work" in North America? Should we dismiss Caucasians' apparent need to relate to a church in which they do not move from the racial majority to the racial minority, with the subsequent loss of political power that follows? If consolidation is a moral imperative, why is it applied to conference structures? Would consolidation advance the work or contribute to the success of mission among the Caucasian group in North America?

With what we now know about history, why would we risk injuring the white work? What we hope is that we could be so Christian and helpful to others that our NAD family would allow us to contribute to a conversation about revitalizing and growing the white work in North America. But such a posture will call for cultural humility. And the first step toward cultural humility is the recognition that whites constitute an ethnic people group. In business language, we presently lack the ability to appreciate market segmentation[114] as a strategy for mission that *includes* whites in the NAD.

John 17:21–23 also implies that the church could easily lapse into power struggles. Jesus' prayer in John 17:21–23 recognizes that as soon as His disciples would lose sight of mission, power struggles for supremacy (James and John), control (Judas), or self-assertion (Peter) would ensue and displace the primary focus. The non-unity of John 17 lay in the disciples' power struggles for supremacy and control. Could it be that this conversation, which is taking so much energy, is nothing other than a deception, if not a distraction, from the work of mission?

Not one critic of Regional conferences has argued that mission among African Americans has not gone and is not going forward. The data on this question is overwhelming. And if it is going forward, what would we like to see beyond that reality? As a church, we have biblical unity, so we have to ask: What else is at issue?

Historically, whites in America have set the norms for America and for the Adventist Church and its institutions. Sociologists call that power *hegemony*, or social dominance. In the family of God, we ought to be able to talk about these and other matters around race and mission even if we disagree. And rather than make pronouncements and calls and demands to dismantle, as some are doing, is it not time that we engage in a loving and honest conversation?

Mission and community

Some who object to present structures base their appeals for dismantling NAD structures on concepts of, and concerns for, community. These perspectives lead to such questions as the following: "Which is more important: mission or community?"

The answer to this question is neither because beneath this question is an assumption that these two values compete with each other in this discussion on structure in the NAD. The true answer is the following: The purpose for community is mission! Community answers the "how," and mission answers the "why" of God's action in the world. Texts, such as Matthew 5:13, 14; 28:17–19; and 1 Peter 2:8, 9, indicate that the community exists to minister, serve, and share God with the world. This relationship between community and mission is summarized in Mrs. White's famous declaration: "The church is God's appointed agency for the salvation of men. It was organized for service, and its mission is to carry the gospel to the world. From the beginning it has been God's plan that through His church shall be reflected to the world His fullness and His sufficiency. The members of the church, those whom He has called out of darkness into His marvelous light, are to show forth His glory."[115] This is why mission is the primary determinant of structural form in historic Adventist understanding.

Regional conferences and restructuring

Some who look at the NAD think that it is time to restructure. They say that we need to dismantle all conferences and start over. They have such questions as the following: "Why don't we dismantle all conferences in the NAD and design new ones?"

The suggestion to disband all conferences is misguided. Why would we need to collapse all conferences and start over? What is the proposed and better replacement? In the interest of input and ownership, should not any new proposal be fully developed and previewed? What are we trying to accomplish? How would mission to target populations be enhanced? What would be the new principles of organization? On what basis would these principles be prioritized? Questions such as these and others should be answered in the setting of an open and constructive conversation between all key stakeholders because Adventist mission in the NAD demands the highest level of due diligence. Some ask, "Did not the General Conference force the conferences in South Africa to merge in 2009? Should not North America be held to the same standard?"

Yes, the General Conference did force a merger in South Africa, but there should not be one standard for all territories.

The General Conference, through the Southern Africa-Indian Ocean Division (SID) and the Southern Africa Union Conference (SAU), demanded that the Transvaal Conference and two congregations of the Cape Conference merge with the Trans-Orange Conference to form a new Northern Conference in November of 2005. The General Conference Working Policy (B65 05), voted in 2005, constituted the policy basis for the Southern Africa Union's decision to merge the fields. In response, six congregations in Transvaal and two in the Cape Conference sued SAU and SID in 2005. The plaintiffs requested that the court declare the reorganization invalid. Their suit was lost. The Free State High Court of South Africa ruled in favor of the GC, SID, and SAU. The High Court ruled that the decision by SAU was not *ultra vires*—outside the power of SAU to merge the conferences in question.

Apartheid laws were implemented in South Africa in 1948. These laws touched every aspect of South African life. They prohibited intermarriage. In 1950, the Afrikaner National Party required blacks and coloreds to carry passbooks that contained photos, birth records, and fingerprints to have access to white areas. This was called the Population Registration Act. In 1951, the Bantu Authorities Act created "homelands" to which blacks were relegated and denationalized blacks' citizenship. The premise was that black South Africans would lose their citizenship in South Africa and become citizens of their homelands. Individuals would have voting rights only in their homeland. Africans needed passports to enter South Africa. Apartheid resulted in the totalitarian oppression of the black majority in South Africa.

But between 1948 and 1992, blacks and coloreds protested. International communities declared embargoes. International companies increasingly refused to do business in South Africa. The United Nations passed declarations condemning the apartheid government. When apartheid ended in 1994 with open, national elections, the newly formed African National Congress government worked aggressively to dismantle the oppressive and painful legacy of apartheid in South Africa. The black-majority South African government was understandably critical toward any and all organizations that held on to what it deemed apartheid-like institutions. The government's critical and condemnatory stance toward the Southern Africa Union's black, colored, and white conferences drove the merger. A missiological determination was made by the General Conference, SID, and SAU leadership—the mission of the Adventist Church would be *hindered* by having a white Afrikaner conference in a consolidated SAU. The decision of SAU to consolidate conferences was prompted because of the stance of the South African government toward apartheid and its symbolic legacy in South Africa. The decision was limited to conference structures and did not extend to local churches.

The move to consolidate conferences was a response to the South African government's negative perception of faith-based organizations that were slow to support the dismantling of apartheid. The SAU decision did not create an integrated SDA church but a consolidated conference structure. The General Conference or the Southern Africa Union never mandated that local churches were to merge in the name of "unity." It was also determined by the Adventist leadership in South Africa that the consolidation of conference structures was in the interest of avoiding misunderstanding in postapartheid South Africa. Interestingly, the Adventist churches in South Africa continue to function based on cultural particularity.

Should the same South African standard apply to North America? It could—but only if we choose to confuse unity with uniformity. The principles outlined in the *Principles, Possibilities, and Limits of Flexibility in the Design of Seventh-day Adventist Organizational Structure* report to the Commission on Ministries, Services, and Structures state very clearly that context, geographical location, and a host of other variables support contextual flexibility in organizational design. Thus, the claim that Regional conferences and state conferences constitute "Adventist apartheid" is without merit.

> As individuals, we need to minister to everyone within our sphere of influence, regardless of race, class, culture, or gender. Is not this the lesson taught in the parable of the good Samaritan?

The situation in North America is different. Unlike in South Africa, there is no pressure from the United States government to dismantle race, culture, nationality, or gender-specific organizations and structures unless they are in violation of US civil rights laws. We have already pointed to examples of such structures. Further, one would have to assume that hostility and antipathy, not mission, are the drivers of Regional conferences. In short, our context and history in North America are different from South Africa. The NAD calls for different organizational strategies and tactics in reaching its diverse people groups. And we pray for the rapid advancement of the work in South Africa.

Finally, we address the question, "Does mission particularity mean that individuals must focus only on people of their own race?"

Not at all. The New Testament contains numerous examples of cross-cultural witnessing. In this discussion on structure, we are talking about institutionalized corporate responsibility for people groups. As individuals, we need to minister to everyone within our sphere of influence, regardless of race, class, culture, or gender. Is not this the lesson taught in the parable of the good Samaritan?

Summary findings

Through our biblical, theological, and missiological analysis of Scripture and Adventist history and present organizational policy, we conclude the following:

1. From a responsible reading of Scripture, Adventist organizational history, and present policy, we affirm that the Bible prescribes no single organizational structure for the people of God to replicate. Thus, eclectic readings of the Scriptures against a particular structural configuration are applied inappropriately.

2. Texts such as John 17:21; Ephesians 2:14, 15; or Galatians 3:26, 27 do not prescribe a particular structural design. Any alleged "biblical" unity that demands structural singularity or consolidation in the NAD represents a reading Scripture through eisegesis. Paul's "body" theology of Romans 12 and 1 Corinthians 12 demonstrates the principle that individuation, whether personal or structural, with unity by mission is encouraged.

3. The assertion that theological or ecclesiastical unity is violated by the existence of mission-particularized structures such as Regional conferences (or Women's Ministries departments, Youth Ministries departments, Korean Ministries, Disability Ministries, etc.) cannot be credibly supported in light of a biblically grounded definition of unity.

4. In SDA ecclesiology, eschatology drives mission, and mission determines structural form. It is the urgency of the SDA message that impels the ministries of Regional conferences to evangelize the 37.6

million African Americans in the United States.

5. The evident supervening Providence that attended the creation of regional structures voids the pejorative labels applied to Regional conferences. These labels are unfortunate, unwarranted, divisive, and an impediment to genuine conversation.

6. Conference structures are not impediments to visible, tangible witness in our communities and country. Witness in communities is carried out every week through the ministries of local Adventist congregations to their communities. It is not the homogeneity or heterogeneity of a congregation that advances or hinders witness; it is whether said congregation loses itself in service to the local community.

7. Ellen White's nineteenth-century admonition to anticipate a "better way" methodology was realized in the twentieth century. The "better way" occurred in the leadership decisions made regarding the Negro work of the Adventist Church between 1891 and 1962. First, in 1909 intentional institutionalization of mission occurred with the organization of the Negro Department. In 1944, the mission focus on African Americans was advanced through the creation of conferences entrusted with authority and responsibility for SDA mission to America's then 12 million African Americans. Third, in 1965, because of the equal rights movements of the 1950s and '60s within and outside of the church, Adventists declared all institutions in the NAD desegregated. Thus, black and white Adventists were liberated to voluntarily unite in worship, mission, and service on a shoulder-to-shoulder basis. The mandatory separation issue was finally addressed and abolished by the corporate church.

Conclusion

If we wish to discuss more effective structures for accomplishing the mission to black America within the polity of the Seventh-day Adventist Church, that conversation is welcomed. But it is disingenuous at worst, and counterproductive at best, to selectively label Regional conferences as examples of disunity and organizational segregation while overlooking other mission particularized structures in the NAD. If there is a more effective structure to facilitate mission to the 37.6 million African Americans in North America, then that structure should be brought forward for discussion. But the assertion that Regional conference structures represent disunity and segregation has neither a biblical nor a missiological basis.

Leslie N. Pollard, PhD, DMin, MBA

Leslie Nelson Pollard serves as the eleventh president of Oakwood University in Huntsville, Alabama. President Pollard brings an extensive education to his service and calling. He earned a Bachelor of Arts degree from Oakwood University (1978), a Master of Divinity degree from Andrews University Seventh-day Adventist Theological Seminary (1983), and a Doctor of Ministry degree in Preaching and Worship from Claremont School of Theology (1992). He also holds an MBA degree from La Sierra University and a PhD in New Testament from Andrews. Besides his administrative and scholarly endeavors, he lectures internationally in the areas of leadership and mission.

---

1. The North American Division (NAD) is one of thirteen world divisions of the General Conference of Seventh-day Adventists. It consists of Bermuda, Canada, the French possession of Saint Pierre and Miquelon, the United States of America, Johnston Island, Midway Islands, and all other islands of the Pacific not attached to the other twelve divisions. Organized in 1913, as of June 30, 2020, the NAD numbered 5,635 churches with a membership of 1,263,064 and a general population of 368,554,000 persons. Within the United States are 58 conferences, organized into nine unions and one mission. Of the fifty-eight US conferences, nine are Regional conferences. For more, see https://www.adventistyearbook.org/entity?EntityID=14197.

2. Regional conferences describe the nine geographical units of the SDA organization in North America which house the predominately African American (black) churches in their respective union territories. The General Conference Spring Council voted on April 10, 1944, to authorize the creation of Regional conferences. At the time Regional conferences were created, the 17,891 black members of the Adventist Church were spread across 233

congregations. More information is available at the General Conference Online Archives in the document about the Regional conferences that begins with "Officers North American Colored Department—1945" at https://documents.adventistarchives.org/Resources /RegionalConf/RCO-02.pdf.

Organized on September 26, 1944, with 2,260 colored believers, Lake Region was the first Regional conference to be organized. The most recent Regional conference, Southeastern, was organized in 1981. Regional conferences today number a membership of approximately 250,000 members. While the primary target population is the 37.6 million African Americans, the Office of Regional Ministries reports that Regional conferences also include 70 nonblack congregations that have voluntarily united within their fellowship. Regional conferences are organizational units in every union of the NAD except the North Pacific and Pacific Unions. According to the *Seventh-day Adventist Encyclopedia*, 1192, "The Regional conferences were formed in the hope that the new organizations might, with concentration on work within a specific ethnic group, achieve greater results in a shorter space of time than would be achieved under the previously existing organizations." Don F. Neufeld, *Seventh-day Adventist Encyclopedia*, rev. ed., vol. 10 of the Commentary Reference Series (Washington, DC: Review and Herald®, 1976), s.v. "Regional Affairs, Office of, and Regional Conferences."

For detailed histories that chronicle the creation of Regional conferences, see Roy Branson, "Adventism's Rainbow Coalition," in *Make Us One*, ed. Delbert Baker (Boise, ID: Pacific Press®, 1995), 75–80; George Knight, *Organizing to Beat the Devil: The Development of Adventist Church Structure* (Hagerstown, MD: Review and Herald®, 2001), 145–150, and R. W. Schwarz, *Light Bearers to the Remnant* (Mountain View: Pacific Press®, 1979), 564–570.

3. David K. Penno, "An Investigation of the Perceptions of Clergy and Laity Concerning Race-Based Organizational Segregation in the Southern Union Conference of Seventh-day Adventists" (PhD diss., Andrews University, 2009), i, ii, iii, etc. One feature of Penno's dissertation that raises a crucial methodological question is the failure to define the key word in his title—*segregation* (note the absence of a definition on pages 12–14). This reader could locate no place in the research where this core term was explicated. Penno's apparent nontechnical use of the term *segregation* raises serious methodological questions that bias his investigation. Under the accepted and common definition of *segregation*, Penno's claim that the SDA Church maintains a "racially segregated organization" (page 2) cannot be substantiated.

4. David Person, "Adventist Apartheid," online letter to the editor, *Adventist Review*, http://www.adventistreview.org/article.php?id=660 (web page discontinued).

5. Samuel Koranteng-Pipim, "Separate Black and White Conferences—Part 1: The Sin We Don't Want to Overcome," Dr. Pipim, accessed August 9, 2021, http://www.drpipim .org/church-racism-contemporaryissues-51/97-separate-black-and-white-conferences -part-1.html.

6. See post on July 4 from "explorer" at http://www.atoday.com/add-your-name-petition (web page discontinued).

7. h0bbes, October 16, 2006, reply to comment posted by Trevan Osborn, October 14, 2006, on "The Beginning of Regional Conferences in the US III," Hobbes Place (blog), September 5, 2006, http://h0bbes.wordpress.com/2006/09/05/the-beginning-of-regional -conferences-in-the-us-iii/.

8. h0bbes, May 8, 2008, reply to comment posted by Stefan, May 8, 2008, on "The Beginning of Regional Conferences in the US III."

9. See "SDA Racially Divided Conferences: The Lingering Evil in SDA Divided

Conferences," *Theological Views*, accessed August 9, 2021, http://njkproject.blogspot
.com/2009/12/sda-racially-divided-conference.html.

10. David Williams, "The Right Thing to Do: A Divided Church and What to Do
About It," *Adventist Review*, February 20, 1997, 26. One weakness in Williams's proposal is
the assertion that the primary organizing principle of a new conference structure should be
equality. Understandably, within the canon of weighted social values, any value other than
equality, tolerance, diversity, etc. sounds like social heresy to modern ears. But the selection
of this value fully reflects our modern consciousness. For Adventist pioneers, mission was
the primary value within the eschatological community and the *primary* determinant of
structural form. See section on Adventist pioneers and structure.

11. William Johnsson, "Four Big Questions," *Adventist Review*, May 25, 2006, http://
www.adventistreview.org/article.php?id=538.

12. Johnsson, http://www.adventistreview.org/article.php?id=538.

13. Frederick A. Russell, "The Obama Message," *Adventist Review*, February 19, 2008,
https://www.adventistreview.org/2008-1505-17. Russell is quick to add in his piece that he
believes that more than nine conferences are "racially defined." He does not elaborate on
how or whether "racially segregated" differs from "racially defined" conferences.

14. See *Adventist Today* online petition at http://www.atoday.com/add-your-name-
petition (web page discontinued). Interestingly, while the petition names both black and
white conferences, much of the most heated rhetoric is directed toward the existence of
Regional conferences. Examples may be seen at the website.

15. It should be recognized that in the NAD, there is no official designation "state conference." Non-Regional conferences are simply referred to as "conferences."

16. See Adventist News Network at http://news.adventist.org/2009/09/lets-talk-encore
-dc.html (web page discontinued). Paulsen was questioned regarding the validity of the
continued existence of Regional conferences. Agreeing with the questioner, he was quoted
as follows: "Tell leaders you think the reasoning behind regional conferences is no longer
valid. I also tell them, but it is good if they hear it from you as well." Elder Paulsen did not
detail or describe the "thinking" referenced in his statement.

17. Dwight Nelson, "The Truth in Black and White," Pioneer Memorial Church, Andrews University, January 16, 2010, https://www.pmchurch.tv/service/2010/01/16/truth
-black-white.

18. *Encyclopaedia Britannica Online*, s.v. "racial segregation," accessed August 10, 2010,
https://www.britannica.com/topic/racial-segregation.

19. In the best-selling business work on organizations and structure, authors Lee Bolman and Terrence Deal assert that structure is "a blueprint for formally sanctioned expectations and exchanges among internal players (executives, managers, employees) and external
constituencies (such as customers . . . and clients). Like an animal's skeleton or a building's
framework, structural form both enhances and constrains what an organization can accomplish." See Lee G. Bolman and Terrence E. Deal, *Reframing Organizations: Artistry, Choice,
and Leadership*, 5th ed. (San Francisco, CA: Jossey-Bass, 2013), 46, 47. They also argue
that "clear, well-understood goals, roles, and relationships and adequate coordination are
essential to performance." Bolman and Deal, 46. Adventist writer William Johnsson writes,
"Structures aren't necessarily good or evil: they may become bureaucratic, an end in themselves, and a drag on innovation; but they also provide *the essential framework for continuity
and concerted action*" (emphasis added). See *The Adventist Review*, November 1997, 17.

20. Ellen G. White writes, "The unity that exists between Christ and His disciples does
not destroy the personality of either. In mind, in purpose, in character, they are one, but

not in person. By partaking of the Spirit of God, conforming to the law of God, man becomes a partaker of the divine nature. Christ brings His disciples into a living union with Himself and with the Father. Through the working of the Holy Spirit upon the human mind, man is made complete in Christ Jesus." "Ellen G. White, Comments—John," in *Seventh-day Adventist Bible Commentary,* ed. Francis D. Nichol, vol 5 (Washington, DC: Review and Herald®, 1980), 1148.

21. "The book of Acts shows that homes (Acts 5:42; 16:32; 18:7–8), synagogues (Acts 9:20; 13:5; 17:1; 19:8), and the Temple (5:20; 5:42) were all centers of evangelistic preaching where unbelievers could hear the gospel. The organizational structures of such places where unbelievers gathered do not have any necessary link with the structure of the local NT church." David W. Miller, "The Uniqueness of New Testament Church Eldership," *Grace Theological Journal* 6, no. 2 (1985): 326.

22. Andrew Mustard, *James White and Organization* (Berrien Springs, MI: Andrews University Press, 1985); Barry Oliver, *SDA Organizational Structure: Past, Present and Future* (Berrien Springs, MI: Andrews University Press, 1989); Knight, *Organizing to Beat the Devil*; Knight, "Organizing for Mission: The Development of Seventh-day Adventist Organizational Structure," http://www.adventist.org/world_church/commission-mission -services-structures/ (web page discontinued). For an anthology of documents that contribute to a better understanding of the historical and contextual currents behind the formation of Regional conferences, see Delbert W. Baker, comp., *Telling the Story: An Anthology on the Development of the Black SDA Work* (Loma Linda, CA: University Printing Services, 1996), 2–73.

23. *Principles, Possibilities and Limits of Flexibility in the Design of Seventh-day Adventist Organizational Structure,* Report to the Commission on Ministries, Services, and Structures, October 4–6, 2006. This commission, organized in 2005, was tasked as follows: "Research and evaluate, in the light of denominational mission and unity, the necessity, efficiency, and effectiveness of current denominational structure." Report is available at http://www.adventist.org/world_church/commission-ministries-services-structures/ (web page discontinued).

24. Knight, "Organizing for Mission," 1. Knight's assessment is accepted with one caveat: whether Adventists are more structured than United Methodists is an open question. See the United Methodist Church's description of their own structure and organization at http://www.umc.org/site/c.lwL4KnN1LtH/b.1720695/k.4FEC/Structure __Organization_O.

25. For example, George Storrs asserted the classic anti-organization statement representing the hostility of many of the Millerite Adventists in the words "No church can be organized by man's invention but what it becomes Babylon *the moment it is organized!*" See George Storrs, "Come Out of Her My People," *Midnight Cry,* February 15, 1844, 238.

26. Note the following: "With the rapid increase in the number of adherents in the 1850s, several problems arose that brought into sharp focus the need of the church for a name and a corporate existence: the legal problems of holding church property and other assets (originally owned by individuals); the growing need for selecting, directing, and supporting a ministry; and the necessity of controlling personal ambition, fanaticism, and offshoot movements." See Don F. Neufeld, ed., *Seventh-day Adventist Encyclopedia,* 2nd rev. ed., vol. 11 of the Commentary Reference Series (Hagerstown, MD: Review and Herald®, 1996), s.v. "Organization, Development of, in the Seventh-day Adventist Church."

27. James White, "Yearly Meetings," *Advent Review and Sabbath Herald,* July 21, 1859, 68.

28. Oliver, *SDA Organizational Structure*, 274–280.

29. For an extended description and discussion of this organizational controversy, see Oliver, 184–201.

30. After Jones and his colleagues reached their conclusions, Ellen White's declaration that "it is not wise to choose one man as president of the General Conference" was especially taken out of context. See Ellen G. White, *Special Testimonies for Ministers and Workers*, no. 8 (College View, Nebraska: College Press, 1897), 29.

31. Oliver, *SDA Organizational Structure*, 346, 347; *Principles, Possibilities, and Limits* report, 5; Knight, *Organizing to Beat the Devil*, 169.

32. See summary of the Annual Council's acceptance of the report on the Adventist News Network at http://news.adventist.org/2007/10/church-structure-to-be-flexible -reflect-local-ees.html (web page discontinued).

33. *Principles, Possibilities, and Limits* report, 2–4.

34. See Leslie Pollard, "The Function of *Loipos* in Contexts of Judgment and Salvation in the Book of Revelation" (PhD diss., Andrews University, 2007), 132–165. In this research, Pollard shows that remnant self-consciousness is intimately tied to the missional identity of God's people.

35. Ellen G. White, *The Acts of the Apostles* (Mountain View, CA: Pacific Press®, 1911), 9.

36. A sense of urgency characterizes Ellen White's call to the Adventist Church of the nineteenth century. Examples include,

We are living in the time of the end. . . .
The condition of things in the world shows that troublous times are right upon us.

And "Unmistakable evidences point to the nearness of the end." Ellen G. White, *Testimonies for the Church*, vol. 9 (Mountain View, CA: Pacific Press®, 1948), 11, 25.

37. "The main theological pillar undergirding Adventist church structure is eschatology. Mission is an outgrowth of eschatology since Adventism believes that the message of the three angels must be preached to all the world before the end of time." Knight, "Organizing for Mission," 47.

38. See Ángel Manuel Rodríguez, ed., *Toward a Theology of the Remnant* (Hagerstown, MD: Review and Herald®, 2009). This book is a compilation of the finest Seventh-day Adventist scholarship on the remnant concept as it relates to the witness of the Scriptures. While *Toward a Theology of the Remnant* avoids an offensive dogmatism, it is clearly affirmative on the application of remnant self-consciousness to the SDA Church and what that self-consciousness means for SDA mission.

39. She wrote in 1909, "Let the colored people work chiefly for those of their own race." White, *Testimonies*, vol. 9, 206.

40. Oliver, *SDA Organizational Structure*, 355. What is curious in Oliver's assessment, and possibly an oversight, is that he does not consider any decisions regarding structure beyond 1903. The creation of Regional conferences is an "Exhibit A" of the structural adaptation that he is arguing for in the SDA Church.

41. See the statistical data referenced in Henry E. Felder, "An Analysis of Seventh-day Adventist Regional Conferences and Economic Development 1950-2008" (unpublished paper presented to the 2010 Regional Conference Caucus in Orlando, Florida, January 22, 2010), 6. African Americans represent approximately 13 percent of the general United States population, but 40 percent of the North American Division. There are no comparable numbers in any other institution or industry in American life. For instance, in schools

of medicine in the US, African Americans represent about 5 percent to 6 percent of all medical school matriculants. In schools of dentistry, the number is 4 percent. In schools of engineering, it is 3 percent. Based on the dramatic financial and numerical growth of the African American Adventist population, it could be successfully argued that the creation of Regional conference structures is the single most successful missional innovation ever undertaken in the North American Division.

42. See the paper by Willie Oliver regarding the sociological situation of African Americans.

43. For a helpful discussion of the "people group" concept, see Reinder Bruinsma, "Missionaries, Go Home! Are Cross-Cultural Missions Still Valid?" in *Adventist Mission in the 21st Century*, ed. Jon Dybdahl (Hagerstown, MD: Review and Herald®, 1999), 41. Bruinsma follows an evangelical definition of a people group: "a significantly large grouping of individuals who perceive themselves to have a common affinity for one another, because of their shared language, religion, ethnicity, residence, occupation, class or caste, situation, or combination of these."

44. Ellen G. Whites writes, "Unity with Christ establishes a bond of unity with one another. This unity is the most convincing proof to the world of the majesty and virtue of Christ, and of His power to take away sin." Ellen G. White Comments—John," in *Seventh-day Adventist Bible Commentary*, 5:1148.

45. In consulting thirty-eight major works, I found no commentator who linked John 17:21–23 to a mandate for a particular type of structure. What they did see was a call to cease the personal striving for supremacy that defined the disciples and an invitation to share His glory, the glory of self-abnegating and self-sacrificial service.

46. For instance, the 2010 *Seventh-day Adventist Yearbook* online acknowledged eighteen mission-particularized ministries listed as official units of the NAD organization, e.g. Asian/Pacific Ministries, Czech Ministries, Deaf Ministries, Disabilities Ministries, Ghanaian Ministries, Greek Ministries, Haitian Ministries, Hispanic Ministries, Hungarian Ministries, Jewish Ministries, Korean Ministries, Muslim Ministries, Native-American Ministries, and a number of others. These individuated ministries are unified around a common purpose while being configured to meet particular demographic groups.

47. See Daniel Overdorf, *Applying the Sermon: How to Balance Biblical Integrity and Cultural Relevance* (Grand Rapids, MI: Kregel Academic and Professional, 2009), 77–80. Overdorf describes the mistakes that preachers often make by recruiting texts and assigning them to one's personal perspectives. He outlines the difference between a number of "application" heresies, e.g. spiritualizing, moralizing, patternizing, trivializing, and normalizing. In relationship to the case raised by the question, Overdorf classifies this case as moralizing. He explains that

> moralizing is drawing moral exhortations from a text that go beyond a text's intention. . . .
> . . . Moralizing often treats possible implications (good advice) as necessary implications (thus saith the Lord). Overdorf, 77, 78.

48. Francis D. Nichol, ed., *The Seventh-day Adventist Bible Commentary*, vol. 5 (Hagerstown, MD: Review and Herald®, 2002), 1053. Also, "because Jesus is one with his Father, and believers are one with the Father and the Son, there should be no room for rivalry and faction." A. Knowles, *The Bible Guide* (Minneapolis, MN: Augsburg: 2001), 524.

49. Overdorf, *Applying the Sermon*, 77, 78. It should be noted that some simply assume

and teach that the highest and best expression of congregational life is multicultural and multiracial. However, these have yet to make a compelling biblical case that proves this contention. And where they can point to examples of what they consider New Testament evidence for multiracial and multicultural local congregations, they generally fail to show that the example cited in Acts 13 or Ephesians 2 or Romans 16 is prescriptive for all local congregations. One can read these passages and get to structural prescription only through what Overdorf identifies as the "application heresy" of patternizing.

50. In a recent publication, Calvin Rock presents a carefully researched and reasoned case for unity in diversity. See Calvin Rock, "Regional Conferences: An Exhibition of Unity in Diversity," *Regional Voice—2010 Special General Conference Issue*, 8–10. In this piece, he illustrates missiological insights with relevant sociological data and examples.

51. An example of the faulty assumption that problematizes diversity itself can be seen in Bruce Milne, *Dynamic Diversity: Bridging Class, Age, Race and Gender in the Church* (Downers Grove, IL: IVP Academic, 2007), 23, 25. For Milne, the Christian church is the "new humanity, in which not only racial diversity but every other major human diversity is both confronted and overcome." This is a flawed assumption because it is grounded in a rejection of diversity. Milne fails to notice that in Pauline perspective, both individual and group diversity is presented as a resource for mission and community. Leslie Pollard develops and presents an original theology of diversity from the Pauline perspective that exposes how the popular fallacy of diversity rejection, diversity blindness, or indifference toward diversity works against effective mission and fellowship in his presentation given at the North American Division's Summit on Race and published as Leslie Pollard, "What Do We Do With Differences?" *Adventist Review*, November 2, 2000, https://www.adventist review.org/archives/2000-1549/story1.html

52. For a broader development of diversity as a resource for mission, see Leslie Pollard, "Culture Matters," *Adventist Review*, December 2, 2004, https://www.adventistreview.org /archives/2004-1506/story1.html.

53. Donald McGavran observed a sociological phenomenon that he famously summa-rized in 1990: "People like to become Christians without crossing racial, linguistic, or class barriers." Donald McGavran, *Understanding Church Growth*, 3rd ed. (Grand Rapids, MI: Eerdmans, 1990), 163. However, there are those who dissent with the church growth movement's description of this "homogeneous unit principle." See C. René Padilla, "The Unity of the Church and the Homogeneous Unit Principle," *International Bulletin of Missionary Research* 6, no. 1 (January 1982):23–30.

54. *Encyclopaedia Britannica Online*, s.v. "racial segregation," accessed August 10, 2021, https://www.britannica.com/topic/racial-segregation.

55. We note with some curiosity in the recent dissertation of Penno from Andrews University, the most crucial term in his title, *segregation*, is not defined. See his list of defi-nitions in Penno, "Race-based Organizational Segregation," 12–14.

56. See Harold Peters, "What's Taking So Long?" letter to the editor, *Adventist Review*, March 11, 2008, https://www.adventistreview.org/archive-1704.

57. Ellen G. White, *Education* (Mountain View, CA: Pacific Press®, 1903), 173.

58. Ellen G. White, *Life Sketches of Ellen G. White* (Mountain View, CA: Pacific Press®, 1915), 196.

59. See the chronicling of this history in George Knight, *A User-Friendly Guide to the 1888 Message* (Hagerstown, MD: Review and Herald®, 1998).

60. For a description of the challenges of this era, see Richard W. Schwarz, *John Harvey Kellogg: Pioneering Health Reformer* (Hagerstown, MD: Review and Herald®, 2006), 178ff.

61. See Richard A. Schaeffer, *Legacy: Daring to Care, Centennial Edition—1905–2005* (Loma Linda, CA: Legacy, 2005), 139, 140.

62. The reader should be aware that there were, in fact, two competing streams of thought within the African American community relative to the Regional conference idea. There were those voices, as early as Elder C. M. Kinney in 1891 and as late as 1929 through Elder J. K. Humphrey, who had been seeking conferences as the natural outgrowth of the success of the 1909 Negro Department, headed by Elder William Green (see the General Conference Executive Committee Minutes, April 29, 1929, 838, 839). There were also those African Americans who sought integration into the existing structure. By 1944, the issues had collided in the incident with Mrs. Lucy Byard. For a summary of the racial tensions between the years 1891 and 1944, see Knight, *Organizing to Beat the Devil*, 145–149.

63. From "Actions of the Spring Meeting of the General Conference Committee," April 10–16, 1944, 15, 16.

64. In an enlightening distillation of the race doctrine of this period, Gunnar Myrdal summarized the social construction of race in America during this period with six propositions:

(1) The Negro people belongs to a separate race of mankind.

(2) The Negro race has an entirely different ancestry [than white people and cannot be related to white people in any way].

(3) The Negro race is inferior [to the white race] in as many capacities as possible.

(4) The Negro race has a place in the biological hierarchy somewhere between the white man and the anthropoids.

(5) The Negro race is so different in both ancestry and characteristics that all white peoples in America . . . can be considered a homogeneous race.

(6) The individuals in the Negro race are comparatively similar to one another and, in any case, . . . than to any white man.

From Gunnar Myrdal, *The Negro Problem and Modern Democracy: An American Dilemma*, vol. 1 (New York: Harper Torch Book, 1944), 103, 104.

65. As an illustration of the depth of the racial challenges of SDA leadership during the first seventy years of the twentieth century, Frank Hale documents the resistance to integration of SDA facilities up to and including the 1962 General Conference Session in San Francisco. SDA leadership was public in its criticism of the faith-based communities who participated in the March on Washington on August 28, 1963. Into the 1960s, key SDA educational and ecclesiastical institutions had not integrated. At San Francisco, the issue of desegregation in the SDA Church was prompted by the involvement of the national press. See Frank W. Hale Jr., *Angels Watching Over Me* (Nashville, TN: James C. Winston, 1996), 157–211.

66. And what we call tolerance may be transient. Ellen G. White believed that there would always be a work that only blacks could do for other blacks. Note her comment in *Testimonies*, vol. 9, 207, 208: "The colored ministers should make every effort possible to help their own people understand the truth for this time. As time advances, *and race prejudices increase*, it will become almost impossible, in many places, for white workers to labor for colored people" (emphasis added).

67. See the insightful analysis and comparison of Regional conferences and the United Methodist Church's Central Jurisdiction by Alfonzo Greene Jr., "Regional Conferences in the Seventh-day Adventist (SDA) Church Compared With United Methodist Central Jurisdiction/Annual Conferences With White SDA Conferences, From 1940–2001" (PhD diss., Loyola University Chicago, 2009), 352–356. Greene shows the impact of

assimilation in the name of unity on the United Methodist Church in the history of the dismantling of the Central Jurisdiction. He carefully documents how the assimilation model exacted a high cost to the UMC's black membership.

68. For an example of the racial situation of the nineteenth-century SDA Church, see Douglas Morgan, *Lewis C. Sheafe: Apostle to Black America* (Hagerstown, MD: Review and Herald®, 2010), 279–311. Lewis C. Sheafe had been a Baptist minister before joining the SDA Church. Possessed of a dynamic personality, he was unable to agree with SDA racial attitudes and practices. Between 1910 and 1915, he was inconsistent in maintaining church membership. He finally left for good. Mrs. White wrote a testimony to him on February 10, 1907 (Letter 44, 1907). In this letter, Ellen White pled with Pastor Sheafe not to be influenced by many of the apostate elements at Battle Creek, some of whom were exacerbating and exploiting his racial struggles in an effort to secure his support for their own purposes.

69. James K. Humphrey was a native of Jamaica and an ordained Baptist minister before joining the SDA Church. He founded First Harlem SDA Church. By 1920 it had six hundred members. He proposed the formation of a Negro conference as a member of the 1929 GC Commission on the Negro Work. He seceded from the SDA Church after his service on the commission. For an extensive and scholarly treatment of Humphrey's career, see R. Clifford Jones, *James K. Humphrey and the Sabbath-Day Adventists* (Jackson, MS: University Press of Mississippi, 2006).

70. Clifford Jones documents the very difficult and confusing relationship of the Adventist Church to the Negro from 1840 to 1930. See Jones, 82–112. He describes the black experience in Adventism as "a saga of paradox, ambiguity and ambivalence." Jones, 82. Also, Richard T. Schaeffer asserts "Relations between racial and ethnic groups are not like relations between family members. The history of the United States is one of racial oppression." Schaeffer, *Race and Ethnicity in the United States*, 4th ed. (Upper Saddle River, NJ: Pearson Prentice Hall, 2007), 4. This model of social dominance is also true of the racial history of the Seventh-day Adventist Church.

71. As examples, see the "Regional Affairs, Office of, and Regional Conferences," in Neufeld, *Seventh-day Adventist Encyclopedia*, rev. ed. (1976), 1193–1195. See also Samuel Koranteng-Pipim, "Separate Black and White Conferences—Part 1: The Sin We Don't Want to Overcome," Dr. Pipim, accessed August 20, 2021, http://www.drpipim.org /church-racism-contemporaryissues-51/97-separate-black-and-white-conferences-part-1.html.

72. Minister and sociologist Calvin Rock rightly questions this assumption. Rock differentiates between segregation, desegregation, and integration. Note his comment in the *Adventist Review*, "The country and the church should honor the guarantees of 'desegregation' (one's privilege of belonging wherever one wishes) and not feel guilty about the natural associational patterns of the races that make general social 'integration' an illusion. Racism (exclusivity based on attitudes of superiority) is the enemy, not racial association with those of common interests or likenesses." Clearly, for Rock, the opposite of segregation is not integration but *desegregation*. To see the full context of his perspective, see Calvin B. Rock, "Please Relax!" in "Readers Respond to Four Big Questions," *Adventist Review*, August 21, 2006, https://www.adventistreview.org/2006-1522-13.

73. On the contrary, it appears that the apostle ranked certain values over and against their relationship to Christian mission. For example, in his day, slavery and taxation were empire-wide activities of the Roman government. Yet Paul appears to have ranked the abolition of slavery and personal freedom as subordinate to the spreading of the gospel. He urged the return of Onesimus to his master, Philemon. Two realities shaped Paul's view: (1) Slavery was not an impediment to the slave in receiving Christ and (2) his view of an im-

minent *eschaton* i.e., "the time is short." But 1 Corinthians 7:21 also reveals Paul's outlook. If a slave could win his freedom, he should, but Paul did not make it a primary pursuit. He even discouraged the custom of "self sale" in 1 Corinthians 7:23. For more insights into the nature of slavery in the New Testament, see Leslie Pollard, "20th Century Slavery and the New Testament," *Message* magazine, (January/February 1994): 28, 29.

Nineteen centuries after Paul, Ellen White called slavery sin and urged Adventists to resist it. Twenty centuries after Paul, the moral outlook of modern nations was expressed on December 10, 1948, when the United Nations voted its Universal Declaration of Human Rights, which codified the global condemnation of slavery in *Article 4*: "No one shall be held in slavery or servitude; slavery and the slave trade shall be prohibited in all its forms." See http://www.un.org/en/documents/udhr/ (web page discontinued).

74. The Negro had been both betrayed and abandoned between the years 1895 and 1910. The United States' Compromise of 1877 resulted in the North effectively deciding to leave the conquered South to itself and its radically reactionary elements. During this period, disaffected Southerners tormented, terrorized, and executed many recently freed slaves. For a detailed description of the treatment of the Negro during this period, see Ronald Graybill, *E. G. White and Church Race Relations* (Washington, DC: Review and Herald®, 1970), 17–34.

75. For a thoughtful treatment of Ellen White's relationship to the nineteenth-century concept of the color line, see Ciro Sepúlveda, *Ellen White on the Color Line: The Idea of Race in a Christian Community* (Biblos Press, 1997), 25–39. Here Sepúlveda outlines the role of the color line in the SDA Church and general society during this period. See also Roy Graham, *Ellen G. White: Co-founder of the Seventh-day Adventist Church* (New York: Peter Lang, 1985), 247–249 for how E. G. White moderated the racial debate in three ways through her leadership. First, she declared that there was no superior or inferior race. Second, she reminded the church, especially the Northern SDA Church, that it was the collective responsibility of the entire nation to make restitution to the formerly enslaved Negro. Third, she spelled out contextually sensitive recommendations for how SDA workers were to proceed with the work for the Southern field.

76. Note the following passage, written by Mrs. White from Australia, to the members working for the colored (black) believers:

> As time advances, and opposition strengthens, *circumstances warn us that discretion is the better part of valor*. If unwise moves have been made in the work done for the colored people, it is not because warnings have not been given. From Australia, across the broad waters of the Pacific, cautions were sent that every movement must be guarded, that the workers were to make no political speeches, and that the mingling of whites and blacks in social equality was by no means to be encouraged.
>
> In a council meeting held in 1895 at Armadale, a suburb of Melbourne, Victoria, I spoke of these matters, in answer to the inquiries of my brethren, and urged the necessity of caution. I said that perilous times were coming, and that the sentiments that could then be expressed in regard to what should be done along missionary lines for the colored people could not be expressed in the future without imperiling lives. I said plainly that the work done for the colored people would have to be carried on along lines different from those followed in some sections of the country in former years.
>
> Let as little as possible be said about the color line, and let the colored people work chiefly for those of their own race.
>
> In regard to white and colored people worshiping in the same building, this cannot

be followed as a general custom with profit to either party—especially in the South. The best thing will be to provide the colored people who accept the truth, with places of worship of their own, in which they can carry on their services by themselves. This is particularly necessary in the South in order that the work for the white people may be carried on without serious hindrance.

Let the colored believers be provided with neat, tasteful houses of worship. Let them be shown that this is done not to exclude them from worshiping with white people, because they are black, *but in order that the progress of the truth may be advanced* [emphasis added]. Let them understand that this plan is to be followed until the Lord shows us a better way. *Testimonies*, vol. 9, 205–207; emphasis added.

77. Graybill, *White and Church Race Relations*, 110ff.

78. Note Ellen White's statement in *Testimonies*, vol. 9, 204: "The gospel is to be presented to the downtrodden Negro race. But great caution will have to be shown in the efforts put forth for the uplifting of this people. Among the white people in many places there exists a strong prejudice against the Negro race. *We may desire to ignore this prejudice, but we cannot do it. If we were to act as if this prejudice did not exist, we could not get the light before the white people. We must meet the situation as it is and deal with it wisely and intelligently*" (emphasis added). Another passage titled "The Color Line" clearly elucidates Ellen G. White's missiology: "The wise course is the best. As laborers together with God, we are to work *in a way that will enable us to accomplish the most for Him.*" White, *Testimonies*, vol. 9, 215; emphasis added.

79. The topic of Regional conferences came to the floor of the GC Committee's Spring Council held April 8–19, 1944, in Chicago. Twenty-two speakers are on record; seventeen spoke in favor of the proposal; three against; and two sought clarification. For a summary, see Delbert W. Baker "Regional Conferences: 50 Years of Progress" *Adventist Review*, November 2, 1995, 11. The following resolution was passed:

WHEREAS, The present development of the work among the colored people in North America has resulted, under the signal blessing of God, in the establishment of some 233 churches with some 17,000 members; and **WHEREAS**, It appears that a different plan of organization for our colored membership *would bring further great advance in soul-winning endeavors* [emphasis added]; therefore

WE RECOMMEND, That in unions where the colored constituency is considered by the union conference committee to be sufficiently large, and where the financial income and territory warrant, colored conferences be organized. Baker, 14.

80. Notice the language of the General Conference Spring Council, 1944 resolution:

WHEREAS, The present development of the work among the colored people in North America has resulted under the signal blessing of God, in the establishment of some 233 churches with some 17,000 members; and **WHEREAS**, *It appears that a different plan of organization for our colored membership would bring further great advance in soul-winning endeavors*; [emphasis added] therefore

WE RECOMMEND, that in unions where the colored constituency is considered by the union conference committee to be sufficiently large, and where the financial income and territory warrant, colored conferences be organized. Baker, 14.

81. If social context is seriously considered, then interpretations like Knight's can, and

should be, called into question. His assertion reads, "While Black [Regional] conferences were certainly not the ideal, their creation seems to have stimulated the denomination's work among certain segments of North America's Black population." See Knight, *Organizing to Beat the Devil*, 150. However, if the new structure dramatically stimulated and advanced the mission to black America, then why would not that advancement in mission be considered "ideal"? Assessments that are deficient from a missiology viewpoint repeatedly overlook the possibility that God's overarching purpose was realized in the dramatic stimulation and growth of the black work in 1944 and beyond.

Further, two points of rebuttal are appropriate. The first is a clarification of Knight's statement: the financial and statistical growth data shows that with the organization of Regional conferences, a remarkable blessing attended the spread of the SDA message among African Americans in North America. The second point raises a question: Do any scholars question why the request for integration was denied? The fact that the request for integration was denied raises the question of whether integration would have facilitated or inhibited the growth of the work among blacks in America. Dogmatic idealism aside, from a missiology perspective, missional particularity in North America better suited the SDA mission to black America. Again, we see that our history did not have to be perfect to work for God's higher purpose.

82. Greene carefully examines a genuine example of "race-based organizational segregation" in his comparative study of the founding of Seventh-day Adventist Regional conferences in 1944 with the United Methodist Church's 1939 creation of its Central Jurisdiction. First, Greene shows that the UM Central Jurisdiction was racially restricted to black United Methodists because it was built upon the 1896 Supreme Court decision in *Plessey v. Ferguson*. On the contrary, Regional conferences were geographically designated but fully open to any SDA who wished to join any Regional conference congregation in 1944. Black Adventists also were free in 1944 to join any white congregation if they so desired. Second, the racially segregated policy of the Central Jurisdiction was formally adopted into the constitution of the United Methodist Church. Such a policy has never been adopted into the Adventist Church. Third, according to Greene, Elder H. T. Elliot, then associate secretary of the General Conference, studied the operation and configuration of Central Jurisdiction and chose not to recommend it as the model for Regional conferences because Central Jurisdiction was officially segregated. See Greene, "Regional Conferences," 234–236. Note that Thomas E. Frank, United Methodist historian, stated that the Central Jurisdiction "embodied the fatal flaw of an apartheid system, segregation of African American churches into a separate, non-regional (geographical) 'church within a church.' " See Thomas Edward Frank, *Polity, Practice, and the Mission of the United Methodist Church* (Nashville: Abingdon Press, 1997), 26.

83. For an excellent discussion of the difficulty of discussing race, see Paul Wachtel, *Race in the Mind of America: Breaking the Vicious Circle Between Blacks and Whites* (New York: Routledge, 1999), 23–39.

84. Former Secretary of State and Stanford professor of history Dr. Condoleezza Rice, in a March 28, 2008, interview at the White House, identified racism as "America's birth defect." She was asked about the impact of then presidential candidate Obama's landmark speech on race. She said, "Black Americans were a founding population. Africans and Europeans came here and founded this country together—Europeans by choice and Africans in chains. That's not a very pretty reality of our founding. . . . Descendants of slaves did not get much of a head start, and I think you continue to see some of the effects of that. That particular birth defect makes it hard for us to confront it, hard for us to talk about it, and hard for us to realize that it has continuing relevance for who we are today." See Rice's

remarks at "Editorial: Notable Quotables in 2008," *Washington Times,* January 2, 2009, https://www.washingtontimes.com/news/2009/jan/2/notable-quotables-in-2008/.

85. For more on these social realities, see Adalberto Aguirre Jr. and David V. Baker, *Structured Inequality in the United States: Critical Discussions on the Continuing Significance of Race, Ethnicity, and Gender* (Upper Saddle River, NJ: Prentice), 2008, 28–85.

86. See the work on this subject by Michael O. Emerson and Christian Smith, *Divided by Faith: Evangelical Religion and the Problem of Race in America* (Oxford, England: Oxford University Press, 2000). This work, consisting of two thousand telephone interviews and two hundred face-to-face interviews, documents the vast differences in perceptions of race and racism in America as held by black and white evangelicals. While most white evangelicals resolutely did not consider themselves racists, they were among the loudest and most critical voices lifted against the Civil Rights movement. Evangelicals' understandings of individual accountability, gradualism, and nonconfrontation of government left them unable to support the social movement for civil equality. To black evangelicals, this was viewed as complicity with, if not outright support of, racial discrimination.

87. See Knight, *Organizing to Beat the Devil,* 146, 147.

88. The post-1944 struggles for desegregation and access are documented in Frank Hale III, *Out of the Trash Came Truth: The 1962 Challenge of the People, by the People, and for the People Against Racism in the Seventh-day Adventist Church* (Columbus, OH: Hale Publishing, 2007), 7–50. This work contains additional detail not included in Hale's *Angels Watching Over Me.*

89. Cultural cohesion is not segregation but group affinities at work because it is voluntary association around the significant experiences of their lives. For a fascinating discussion of this process, see Beverly Daniel Tatum, *Why Are All the Black Kids Sitting Together in the Cafeteria and Other Conversations About Race* (New York: Basic Books, 2002). While Tatum focuses on identity formation in adolescents, the book has many helpful insights about the role that race plays in group cohesion.

90. Thomas Schreiner, *New Testament Theology: Magnifying God in Christ* (Grand Rapids, MI; Baker, 2008), 714, 715.

91. To better appreciate the racially charged environment and social context in which Mrs. White penned her counsel, a careful and detailed description of the social setting and culture of the nineteenth and early twentieth centuries can be found in Norman Miles, "Tension Between the Races," in *The World of Ellen White,* ed. Gary Land (Hagerstown, MD: Review and Herald®, 1987), 47–60.

92. White, *Testimonies,* vol. 9, 206, 207.

93. For an analysis of the social and cultural context of Mrs. White's General Conference sermon on race and mission, see Leslie Pollard, "The Cross Culture," *Adventist Review,* February 3, 2000, 20–24.

94. See Ronald D. Graybill, "Historical Contexts of Ellen G. White's Statements Concerning Race Relations" (unpublished BD thesis, Andrews University, 1968).

95. Ellen White saw that attempts to better the situation of the colored people of the South were deeply threatened by entrenched prejudice. She wrote, "One of the difficulties attending the work is that many of the white people living where the colored people are numerous are not willing that special efforts should be put forth to uplift them. When they see schools established for them, when they see them being taught to be self-supporting, to follow trades, to provide themselves with comfortable homes instead of continuing to live in hovels, they see the possibility that selfish plans will be interfered with—that they will no longer be able to hire the Negro for a mere pittance; and their enmity is aroused.

They feel that they are injured and abused. Some act as if slavery had never been abolished. This spirit is growing stronger as the Spirit of God is being withdrawn from the world, and in many places it is impossible now to do that work which could have been done for the colored people in past years." White, *Testimonies*, vol. 9, 204, 205.

96. The 1890s saw increased violence against African Americans. In the decade of the 1890s, 1,691 African Americans were lynched. See Ida B. Wells-Barnett, *On Lynchings* (New York: Humanity, 2002), 201, 202. From 1900 to 1914, more than 1,100 were lynched. See John Hope Franklin and Alfred A. Moss Jr., *From Slavery to Freedom: A History of African Americans,* 8th ed. (New York: Alfred Knopf, 2004), 345.

97. For examples of the malicious treatment white and black Adventists experienced in the Southern field—from shootings to lashings, to burning of church properties during this period, see Graham, *Ellen G. White*, 242–244. An example of the aggressiveness of angry local whites against Adventist believers is seen in the Olvin incident in Calmar, Mississippi, on May 11, 1899. Not only was Mr. Olvin, an African American, attacked by an angry mob of whites because of his cross-racial fraternization, but also his wife was shot while protesting the mob's horsewhipping of Mr. Olvin. See account in Graybill, *Church Race Relations*, 56.

98. Ellen White's mission centrality is evident in the following statement:

I said plainly that the work done for the colored people would have to be carried on along lines different from those followed in some sections of the country in former years.

Let as little as possible be said about the color line, and let the colored people work chiefly for those of their own race. White, *Testimonies*, vol. 9, 206.

Contrast her methodology with the position of Elie Wiesel some seventy-five years later. Wiesel declared: "I swore never to be silent whenever wherever human beings endure suffering and humiliation. We must take sides. Neutrality helps the oppressor, never the victim. Silence encourages the tormentor, never the tormented." "The Nobel Acceptance Speech Delivered by Elie Wiesel in Oslo on December 10, 1986," PBS, accessed August 11, 2021, http://www.pbs.org/eliewiesel/nobel/index.html.

99. See Charles E. Bradford, *Preaching to the Times: The Preaching Ministry in the Seventh-day Adventist Church* (Washington, DC: Review and Herald®, 1975).

100. See Pollard, "What Do We Do With Differences?"

101. For instance, health-care research shows that America is anything but post-racial. IOM researchers concluded that "a large body of research [on health care disparities] reveals that racial and ethnic minorities experience a lower quality of health services, and are less likely to receive even routine medical procedures than are white Americans." The report continues, "African Americans . . . are less likely to receive appropriate cardiac medication . . . or to undergo coronary artery bypass surgery . . . , are less likely to receive peritoneal dialysis or kidney transplantation." By contrast, they are more likely to receive certain less-desirable procedures, such as lower limb amputations for diabetes and other conditions. Brian D. Smedley, Adrienne Y. Stith, and Alan R. Nelson, eds., *Unequal Treatment: Confronting Racial and Ethnic Disparities in Health Care* (Washington, DC: National Academies Press, 2003), 2. Also, more recently, in 2006, a team of researchers concluded: "It is well established that racial-ethnic minorities in the United States have poorer health than whites. The most meaningful summary measure of such disparities is life expectancy. Black and American Indian/Alaskan Native populations have higher rates of age-adjusted and age-specific mortality than other groups." Jeanne Miranda et al., "Reducing Mental Health

Disparities: General Vs. Behavioral Health Policy," MacArthur Foundation, accessed August 11, 2021, https://www.macfound.org/media/files/disparities.pdf, 1.

102. White, *Testimonies*, vol. 9, 195.

103. White, 199.

104. Then Sister White wrote,

> If a colored brother sits by their side [of whites], they will not be offended or despise him. They are journeying to the same heaven, and will be seated at the same table to eat bread in the kingdom of God. . . .
>
> . . . They [blacks] should hold membership in the church with the white brethren. Every effort should be made to wipe out the terrible wrong which has been done them. Ellen G. White, *The Southern Work* (Washington, DC: Review and Herald®, 1966), 14, 15.

105. "In regard to white and colored people worshiping in the same building, this cannot be followed as a general custom with profit to either party—especially in the South. The best thing will be to provide the colored people who accept the truth, with places of worship of their own, in which they can carry on services by themselves. This is particularly necessary in the South in order that the work for the white people may be carried on without serious hindrance." White, *Testimonies*, vol. 9, 206.

106. Ellen G. White, *Testimonies for the Church*, vol. 6 (Mountain View, CA: Pacific Press®, 1948), 339.

107. O. A. Olsen and L. A. Hoopes, "Twenty-sixth Meeting, April 20, 10:30 A. M.," *General Conference Bulletin: Thirty-Fourth Session*, April 22, 1901, 389.

108. White, *Testimonies*, vol. 9, 195.

109. White, 196.

110. White, 196.

111. White, 196.

112. White, 195.

113. Williams, "Right Thing to Do," 26.

114. For an analogy to mission particularity, see "Market Segmentation," an introductory discussion of the concept of market segmentation on the Net MBA website at http://www.netmba.com/marketing/market/segmentation/. Note the following definition: "Market segmentation is the identification of portions of the market that are different from one another. Segmentation allows the firm to better satisfy the needs of its potential customers." "Market Segmentation."

115. White, *Acts of the Apostles*, 9.

CARL MCROY

Afterword

The most disrespected person in America is the black woman. The most unprotected person in America is the black woman. The most neglected person in America is the black woman," Malcolm X famously asserted in a provocative 1962 speech. Yet, black women have often been the most engaged, the most determined, and the most influential in promoting hope, healing, and wholeness in America. I am painfully grateful to Dr. Ramona Hyman for accepting this mantle and founding the African American Healers' Conference. Grateful because we need it. Painfully grateful because we shouldn't.

Since the 2013 African American Healers' Conference at Loma Linda (which serves as the basis of this book), the United States has exposed its urgent need for healing. The malignancy of America's original and recurrent sin has openly metastasized across our governmental, economic, health-care, and religious systems. The COVID-19 pandemic disproportionately sickened and killed black, indigenous, and people of color populations in the United States, yet many in these people groups have vaccine hesitancy partly due to centuries of exploitive and harmful medical experiments on people of color.[1]

Dozens of citizens of color have died at the hands of police while pleading, "I can't breathe."[2] Professional athletes who peacefully protested against this abuse of authority were derided with a crude and profane insult, while white supremacist terrorists were commended as "very fine people."

Minority businesses were an afterthought when billions of dollars in COVID-19 relief were disbursed to keep white-owned businesses afloat.[3] Of course, black female business owners received the worst of this economic gut-punch.[4]

Many state governments have outlawed teaching elements of American history that examine the role racism played in the nation's founding while protecting and perpetuating Confederate monuments and holidays. High-profile seminaries have condemned academic critiques of racism as being more harmful than racism itself while defending the honor of their slave-owning founders.

The whole world's attention was seized on January 6, 2021, as the US Capitol was invaded by hordes of neo-Nazis wearing shirts with genocidal slogans; neo-Confederates parading their symbol of sedition; barbarians defecating in the hallways; vandals looting legislators' desks; paramilitary groups insulting, beating, disarming, tasing, tear-gassing, and trampling police officers; terrorists demanding the hanging of the vice president, for whom they had prepared gallows; and Christian nationalists initiating a prayer-and-praise service after sacking the congressional chambers.

All this with the goal of overturning the 2020 presidential election results. Not all the results, necessarily. Just enough. Mainly the ones from metropolitan areas with high concentrations of people of color, whose votes are historically slandered as invalid for one reason or another. In a parallel move, hundreds of voter suppression laws have recently been introduced to solve the fabricated problem of widespread voter fraud.

This was only the abridged version of what most of us have witnessed through various news outlets and personal experiences. This book looks to the past for reference points to help us navigate contemporary challenges that change as rapidly as social media trends. What do we as Christians, as African Americans, as concerned humans do? How do we promote the healing of so many interconnected, intergenerational, institutional illnesses? How do we address the different camps within the church that have contrary interpretations of everything listed above?

First, become informed through books and conferences such as African American Healers. Second, get involved with conversations and organizations that lead to positive actions. Your head, heart, and hands are needed. You don't need to be an African American to join this healing effort. You don't need professional and academic credentials, like the contributors in this book, to make a difference. You just need to sense that something is broken and people are hurting. Be aware that inaction aids injustice. Be assured that intervention is a vital way to experience God (Isaiah 59:14–16). A good starting place is AfricanAmericanHealers.com and @AAHealers on Twitter, Facebook, and Instagram.

Carl McRoy

Carl McRoy is an ordained minister who currently serves as the director of Literature Ministries for the North American Division of Seventh-day Adventists and is a frequent feature writer for *Message* magazine.

---

1. For more information, see Harriet A. Washington, *Medical Apartheid: The Dark History of Medical Experimentation on Black Americans From Colonial Times to the Present* (New York: Anchor, 2008).

2. Mike Baker et al., "Three Words. 70 Cases. The Tragic History of 'I Can't Breathe,' " *New York Times*, June 29, 2020, https://www.nytimes.com/interactive/2020/06/28/us/i-cant-breathe-police-arrest.html.

3. "Minority-Owned Businesses Were Last in Line to Receive Loans, Latest PPP Data Show," CBS News, January 4, 2021, https://www.cbsnews.com/news/minority-owned -businesses-were-last-to-receive-ppp-loans-adding-to-their-despair/.

4. Alexi McCammond, "COVID-19 Decimated Black Women-Owned Businesses— Ayesha Curry Wants to Change That," NBC News, June 3, 2021, https://www.nbcnews .com/know-your-value/feature/covid-19-decimated-black-women-owned-businesses -ayesha-curry-wants-ncna1269584.

ANDY LAMPKIN, PhD

An Uncritical Postscript

These essays reflect a critical awareness of the complex and enduring issues surrounding race and racism within the Seventh-day Adventist Church and American society. African American Seventh-day Adventists demonstrate their deep commitment to the denomination and Christianity in advocating for and working toward racial and ethnic justice within the church and society. The two sermons, four conference presentations, two invited articles, and afterword included in this book eloquently communicate that African American Seventh-day Adventists have improved their church and society as they practice their faith within the fellowship of the Seventh-day Adventist Church.

Warren's sermon, "Faith Hall of Famers," and Rock's sermon, "Healed by Something Better," were preached as part of a divine worship service at the multicultural Loma Linda University church. Jackson's "Healing Shepherds and the Pastoral Care of African American Religioracial Ills," King's "We, Too, Sing America," Pascal's "Westward Leading," and my own "Repairers of the Breach" initially began as conference presentations as part of a panel of ministers and theologians, which I moderated, intending to explore African American Seventh-day Adventist contributions to the church and society. These presentations were developed into the articles contained in this volume. Pollard's "Conference, Mission, Structure, and Function" and Kyle's "To Dream, to Be, to Act" were invited essays with the goal of adding more perspective to the experiences of African American Seventh-day Adventists as healers in church and society. Finally, McRoy's "Afterword" points us in the direction of the kind of healing work that needs to be done in our contemporary situation of racial and ethnic injustice.

Warren's sermon, "Faith Hall of Famers," opened the conference and raised an important question: Are we there yet? This question is seldom discussed in mixed company among Adventists. The heroes in his sermon are the waves of faith warriors, stalwarts that include those mentioned in Hebrews 11, the Protestant Reformers, the founders of the Seventh-day Adventist Church, and the community of African American Seventh-day Adventist healers. The Adventists he refers to are activists, both past and present, who build up the church. These, according to Warren, are "God-honored champions having 'the faith of Jesus.' " Warren provides an interpretive key for understanding the African American Seventh-day Adventist approach to social justice advocacy work and activism within the church and society—their faith in Jesus.

Rock's sermon, "Healed by Something Better," introduces the reader to the "something better" principle. This principle, according to Rock, is a part of the human condition and has been operative in our nation since its founding. He takes the reader on a journey through the African American experience. He provides descriptive titles for each of his movements, including "Previously Without Hope." Here, he explores the paradox of slaves being brought to this country on ships with suggestive names such as *The Liberty* and *The Good Ship of Jesus* only to be abused, treated like animals, and forced into permanent servitude.

In a section titled "A Glimmer of Hope," he offers insights into slave conversion to Christianity and the birth of Negro spirituals. These are examples of the "something better" principle and the movement toward progress. The final sections, "The Adventist Connection," "The Journey Ahead," and "This Is Personal," explore the activist work of Seventh-day Adventist leaders, black and white.

"This Is Personal," his concluding section, captures the spirit of many African American Seventh-day Adventists who work toward racial and ethnic justice. Rock helps us understand that it's personal for many of us. He notes how his roots run deep into Adventism and America. This is our church, this is our nation, and it's our duty to make them better. When you hope for something better, you don't just wait in anticipation—you actively work to help bring it about. This is the lesson of the Gospels.

King's essay, "We, Too, Sing America," tells of a journey of striving and hope. She is proud of the abolitionist roots and activism of early Seventh-day Adventists. Sojourner Truth and Anna Knight are set apart and admired for their contributions as healers and women in ministry. Truth is celebrated as an operative of the underground railroad, a gifted speaker, and a woman who worked on behalf of the last, the lost, and the least and kept company with dignitaries. Anna Knight is celebrated as an educator, gifted speaker, innovator, and inspiration to women in ministry. King makes an interesting note that the reader should not overlook when discussing Knight—namely, Knight's awareness that Seventh-day Adventists were not saints. This introduces readers to both the hope and the pain that many African American Adventists feel regarding our church's record on racism. Her response is that we must continue to work and to make things better.

King traces the movements of Seventh-day Adventist history and places black women at the forefront of making things better. However, she is concerned that despite all the labor of African American women on behalf of the church, "black women have been left in the kitchen." African American Seventh-day Adventist women confront the "invisibility of black women" and the "double jeopardy" that all black American women face. She concludes her essay on a most provocative note. She says, "African American women will be great in the kingdom because . . . they have been least of all." "But until then," she says, "they'll see how beautiful we are—and be ashamed—we, too, are American."

Jackson's essay, "Healing Shepherds and the Pastoral Care of African American Religioracial Ills," encourages us to think more carefully about our theological commitments. He is worried that some African American clergy members, the healing shepherds, embrace and adopt too quickly "top-down theology." He offers practical theology as an alternative because it grows out of the grass roots. He notes that "when pastors profess to be the spiritual healers of a people and yet fail to take their context of ministry as not only a place to offer service but also as the location for research into the working of God among people today, they ought to be distrusted." This is an explicit acknowledgment of what God is doing among the people in the world today.

Jackson calls for black theologians to reimagine their theological roots. He raises a profound yet uncomfortable question for Seventh-day Adventists: "Why is there not more work among young African American Adventists that tells the story of the Advent movement through the workings of Richard Allen and other captive and free black people who awaited the coming of Christ?" This is a call for an appropriation of black historical and theological resources in African American Seventh-day Adventist theological reflection. This appropriation of African American intellectual resources is required if the African American Seventh-day Adventist Church is going to be, indeed, a healing church. Moreover, this is essential, in Jackson's view, if we are at all serious about multicultural discourse within Adventism—"A people cannot shepherd a multicultural discourse if they are not free to affirm their own culture." What a powerful acknowledgment!

Pollard's essay, "Conference, Mission, Structure, and Function," makes the case for the organizational structural unit affectionally known as regional conferences. Pollard understands something not available to the uninitiated: the Seventh-day Adventist Church is highly structured and institutionalized. This feature of the church cuts two ways. It has contributed to rapid church growth and globally expansive membership and the development and growth of its network of educational and health-care institutions. However, highly centralized bureaucratic institutions, even democratic ones, are susceptible, at times, to failing to meet the needs of the local constituency. Pollard makes clear that the church carries out its mission in the world through its bureaucratic structures. His concern is African American Seventh-day Adventist ministry and the institutional structural contexts in which that work is done. The regional conferences in the North American Division exist as the structural unit to support, develop, and grow healing shepherds and minister to African Americans. Many people struggle with the symbolism of regional conferences— at first glance, it looks like separation of the races. Pollard looks twice and more carefully into what they represent—he does that work for us.

Paschal's essay, "Westward Leading," tells the story of Seventh-day Adventist expansion into western territories. Although stories abound in Seventh-day Adventist literature regarding the move west, few people tell the story that Paschal tells of the black Seventh-day Adventist work in Southern California and the establishment of Berean, the first black church in Los Angeles. Berean and its pastor, Lewis C. Sheafe, were healers who fought against the negative racial attitudes of the time, which were thought to be dehumanizing and subservient. They advocated for the greater inclusion of blacks into the leadership structures of the denomination. Paschal notes that such struggle continues and that black Seventh-day Adventists need to organize and develop a collective agenda around the issues that impact the community we are called to serve—namely, poor quality education, school to prison pipeline, homelessness, and joblessness.

Kyle's essay, "To Dream, to Be, to Act," is perhaps, the most personal and discusses a tension that exists among clergy about how best to define ministry and being a minister. In his view, for too long, black Seventh-day Adventists have focused too narrowly on pastoral ministry, to the chagrin of other legitimate forms of ministry. He recounts his dream of becoming a physician. However, his dream was not well received among his ministerial colleagues. Already an ordained minister, he felt called to the vocation of medicine. He felt chided for daring to dream to become a medical doctor. The vision that he offers to combine church ministries and health ministries is what Seventh-day Adventists have advocated since their inception. His work as a physician at the front lines of reducing health care disparities and promoting health fits within the African American healing motif and pushes us beyond the limits of the status quo both in church ministries and medicine.

McRoy's "Afterword" reminds us of the importance of the kind of work contained in this volume, considering the contemporary situation. He points us in the direction of the contemporary challenges of racism. He raises some questions: What are we to do as committed Christians? And, as African Americans, how do we promote healing among new intergenerational and institutional illnesses? His answer is simple yet, profound—get engaged!

As I reflect on this volume, I am left inspired and hopeful. These authors are ministers, pastors, theologians, and administrators who faithfully serve their church while paying critical attention to the context of their work. In their own ways, they have come to terms with the reality of the practice of racism within the church and society. They are all prisoners of hope and are motivated by their deep faith commitments. Their religious and social conscience allows them to view the progress and accomplishments of African American Seventh-day Adventist activists, in terms of the struggle for civil rights and as the voice crying out in the wilderness. This is deeply personal! Moreover, this is God-inspired work! We, too, are Adventist!